JOURNEYS

Benchmark and Unit Tests

Grade 3

HOUGHTON MIFFLIN HARCOURT
School Publishers

"New Kitten" by Mona Pease, illustrated by Helen Cogancherry from *Ladybug* magazine, August 2004. Text copyright © 2004 by Mona Pease. Illustrations copyright © 2004 by Helen Cogancherry. Reprinted by permission of The Cricket Magazine Group, a division of Carus Publishing Company.

"Lazy Day" by Eileen Spinelli, illustrated by Stephanie Roth from *Highlights for Children* magazine, June 2006. Copyright © 2006 by Highlights for Children, Inc. Reprinted by permission of Highlights for Children, Inc.

Adapted from "The Talking Yam: An African Folktale" by Marilyn Helmer from *chickaDEE* magazine, November 2004. Reprinted by permission of Bayard Presse Canada, Inc.

"Day and Night in the Desert" illustrated by Paige Billin-Frye from *Click* magazine, April 2004. Text copyright © 2004 by Carus Publishing Company. Illustrations copyright © 2004 by Paige Billin-Frye. Reprinted by permission of The Cricket Magazine Group, a division of Carus Publishing Company.

"Rainbow Trout's Colors" by Robert James Challenger, illustrated by Susan Kwas from *chickaDEE* magazine, March 1999. Illustrations copyright © 1999 by Susan Estelle Kwas. Reprinted by permission of Bayard Presse Canada, Inc. and Morgan Gaynin, Inc. on behalf of Susan Estelle Kwas.

Copyright © by Houghton Mifflin Harcourt Publishing Company

All rights reserved. No part of this work may be reproduced or transmitted in any form or by any means, electronic or mechanical, including photocopying or recording, or by any information storage or retrieval system, without the prior written permission of the copyright owner unless such copying is expressly permitted by federal copyright law.

Permission is hereby granted to individuals using the corresponding student's textbook or kit as the major vehicle for regular classroom instruction to photocopy copying masters from this publication in classroom quantities for instructional use and not for resale. Requests for information on other matters regarding duplication of this work should be addressed to Houghton Mifflin Harcourt Publishing Company, Attn: Contracts, Copyrights, and Licensing, 9400 South Park Center Loop, Orlando, Florida 32819.

Printed in the U.S.A.

ISBN-13: 978-0-54-736887-0
ISBN-10: 0-54-736887-9

5 6 7 8 9 10 0982 18 17 16 15 14 13 12 11
4500287606

If you have received these materials as examination copies free of charge, Houghton Mifflin Harcourt Publishing Company retains title to the materials and they may not be resold. Resale of examination copies is strictly prohibited.

Possession of this publication in print format does not entitle users to convert this publication, or any portion of it, into electronic format.

Contents

© Houghton Mifflin Harcourt Publishing Company. All rights reserved.

Name _____ Date _____

Reading

Read the selection. Then read each question that follows it.
Decide which is the best answer to each question.
Mark the space for the answer you have chosen.

The Color Wheel

1   Jaden and Noah were planning to redecorate their bedroom. The brothers were quite excited and ready to make changes, but mostly, they were <u>eager</u> to start painting.

2   "It's going to look so awesome with green walls," said Jaden.

3   "What? Who said anything about green walls?" Noah argued. "I was planning to paint our room red."

4   "Red will look horrible, and besides, green is a much better color," Jaden replied.

5   The boys' smiles disappeared, and frowns started to become visible.

6   "Okay, let's think about this. I'm sure we can decide on a color together," said Noah.

7   "Hey, I have an idea that might be useful. Our art teacher showed us how to use a color wheel, which displays all of the colors of the rainbow. All of the colors are arranged in a circle, and the color wheel shows how new colors are made from mixing certain main colors together. Let's look at a color wheel and see what we can come up with," Jaden suggested.

8   Jaden pulled out a book about art that included a color wheel.

9   "How is that going to help us?" Noah asked.

10   "Well, maybe we'll find another color we both like," Jaden answered.

11   Jaden opened the book to a page with a color wheel on it, and the boys began to study it. They saw that red and green are on opposite sides of the color wheel, which means they are very different from one another. Sometimes colors that are not alike work well together, but they can also be so different that they don't work well together.

© Houghton Mifflin Harcourt Publishing Company. All rights reserved.

12   "Hey, these colors look good together," said Jaden. He pointed to a golden color and a green color. The colors were side by side on the color wheel, but they were not similar.

13   Noah agreed. "But I really do like red," he added.

14   "Well, I like blue as much as I like green. What would happen if we mixed blue and red?" Jaden asked.

15   The boys looked at the color wheel. The color in between red and blue on the wheel was purple. They looked at each other and started to grin.

16   "I think we might have solved our problem," said Jaden.

17   "I think you're right," said Noah.

GO ON ➤

Name _____ Date _____

1 The story is mostly about two brothers who—
- ⬭ cannot get along
- ⬭ decide to paint a bedroom two colors
- ⬭ discuss a problem and work it out
- ⬭ cannot make a decision

2 Which word means the opposite of the word <u>eager</u> in paragraph 1?
- ⬭ Thoughtless
- ⬭ Annoyed
- ⬭ Ready
- ⬭ Unwilling

3 Jaden suggests he and Noah look at a color wheel to—
- ⬭ show Noah what he learned in school
- ⬭ make Noah forget about the problem
- ⬭ find a color they both like
- ⬭ prove green is better than red

4 Where does Jaden find the color wheel?
- ⬭ In his bag
- ⬭ On a shelf
- ⬭ In a book
- ⬭ At school

5 Noah and Jaden will most likely—
- ⬭ keep looking at the color wheel
- ⬭ paint their bedroom blue and red
- ⬭ decide on a color another day
- ⬭ paint their bedroom purple

© Houghton Mifflin Harcourt Publishing Company. All rights reserved.

> **Read the selection. Then read each question that follows it.**
> **Decide which is the best answer to each question.**
> **Mark the space for the answer you have chosen.**

Animal Homes

1 Some animals live in open areas. When they get tired, they just lie down to sleep. Other animals use caves or hollowed out trees as their homes. There are also various animals that are able to build their own homes. Beavers, prairie dogs, alligators, and hornets are several of the animals who build their own places to live.

Beavers

2 Beavers build a home called a lodge. Beavers move slowly on land but are quick in the water, so they build their homes in water to stay safe. Beavers use their four long, sharp, front teeth to cut  down trees. They use trees and branches to make a dam, which blocks the flow of water in a stream and creates a pond. Then beavers build their lodge, which looks like a large pile of sticks and mud, in the pond. Other animals are unable to get inside the lodge because the entrance is under the water. The beavers have a dry place inside the lodge to sleep and eat.

Prairie Dogs

3 Another animal that builds its home is the prairie dog. Prairie dogs are members of the squirrel family, but they do not live in trees. These animals dig tunnels for a place to live. They make what is called a town, which is made of many tunnels and small rooms. Hundreds of prairie dogs live in the town together. They carry grass inside to make comfortable beds. Prairie dogs are <u>secure</u> in their towns because large animals cannot get inside. The towns stay cool on hot days, and they stay warm when it is cold outside.

© Houghton Mifflin Harcourt Publishing Company. All rights reserved.

Alligators

4   Alligators build homes called nests. An alligator nest is built at the edge of the water and is made of grass and mud. Some nests are about three feet high and six feet wide. The female alligator lays her eggs in the nest, which is a very special place because it is built to keep the eggs warm. The female covers the eggs with rotting plants, and these rotting plants make heat.

Hornets

5   Another animal that makes its home in a nest is the hornet. Hornets are flying insects, much like bees. Hornets make big round nests that look like gray balloons. The hornets make the nest by chewing wood that becomes soft and wet. After the pieces of wood dry, they become paper. Inside the nest, there are tiny cups, and the eggs and the young hornets stay in these cups.

6   Animals' homes keep them safe, warm, and dry. Some animals build homes for many of the same reasons that people build homes!

7   Look at the chart to learn about some other types of animal homes.

Places Some Animals Live

Animal	Home	Location
bear	den	in caves or other sheltered places that stay cool
bee	hive	on the ground, in trees, or even in buildings
bird	nest	in trees, on the ground, or even near buildings
mole	ground	burrow, under logs, or rocks
worm	soil or earth	underground

GO ON

© Houghton Mifflin Harcourt Publishing Company. All rights reserved.

6 In paragraph 3, what does the word <u>secure</u> mean?
- ◯ Safe
- ◯ Calm
- ◯ Locked
- ◯ Warm

7 The article is mostly about—
- ◯ how to find a place to rest
- ◯ the different homes animals live in
- ◯ the different ways animals meet their needs
- ◯ how to build a house

8 If another animal chases it, a beaver will most likely—
- ◯ use its sharp teeth to scare it
- ◯ swim underwater to its home
- ◯ swim away to the nearest land
- ◯ make a tall pile of sticks and mud

9 Which section of the article tells you about an animal home that looks like a gray balloon?
- ◯ Beavers
- ◯ Prairie Dogs
- ◯ Alligators
- ◯ Hornets

10 According to the chart, which animal lives in a burrow?
- ◯ Bear
- ◯ Bee
- ◯ Mole
- ◯ Worm

11 According to the chart, which two animals have homes underground?
- ◯ Bees and bears
- ◯ Moles and worms
- ◯ Moles and birds
- ◯ Bees and worms

GO ON ▶

> **Read the selection. Then read each question that follows it.**
> **Decide which is the best answer to each question.**
> **Mark the space for the answer you have chosen.**

New Kitten

by Mona Pease
art by Helen Cogancherry

1   I have a new kitten. He lives at my grandparents' house, but I visit him every weekend.

2   When Grandma told me I could have a kitten, we went shopping for things it would need. We bought a litter box and litter, a soft brush, and some dry kitten food. I picked out a fluffy mouse and a small ball, too. Grandma and Grandpa took me to their neighbors' farm to pick a kitten from their mother cat's litter.

3   There were four kittens left. They were all so cute that we couldn't decide which one to choose, so we stood very still and waited to see which kitten would come to us. A tiger-striped one climbed on my shoe and meowed. We brought him home, and I named him Jethro.

© Houghton Mifflin Harcourt Publishing Company. All rights reserved.

Name _____ Date _____

4   When I picked Jethro up, he purred really loudly. At first, I thought it was his stomach growling! He didn't want to snuggle too long. He wanted to play. He let me carry him around in a basket. Then he played with his ball and batted at his toy mouse. Soon he got tired and fell asleep.

5   Grandma told me that I would take care of Jethro on weekends. Grandma said she would keep the litter box clean, but the rest was up to me. It was my job to keep Jethro's dishes clean and filled with fresh water and food. She said another job was to gently brush him to keep his coat from getting <u>snarled</u>. I promised to take good care of my kitten.

6   One day Grandma and I took Jethro to the veterinarian. That's a special doctor for animals, just like my pediatrician is a special doctor for children. In the car, Jethro rode in a small carrier that looked like a cage. Even though Grandma had put his little mouse inside, Jethro didn't like being closed in. He yowled all the way! When we got to the veterinarian's office, Grandma filled out a paper that told the workers Jethro's name and age and who owned him. She put my name on that line.

© Houghton Mifflin Harcourt Publishing Company. All rights reserved.

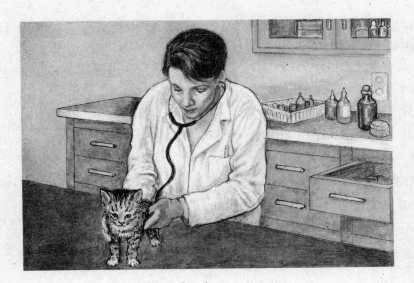

7   The veterinarian listened to Jethro's heart with her stethoscope. She looked at his eyes and in his ears. Uh-oh! She said my kitten had ear mites and gave us some medicine to take home. And then, just like at my pediatrician's, Jethro needed a shot. It was to keep him from getting any bad cat diseases. Jethro meowed, so I guess he didn't like that very much.

8   Now Jethro is home, and Grandpa puts the medicine in his ears every day.

9   Grandma cleans the litter box, and I wash Jethro's dishes and make sure they're full of food and water. I don't mind all the work I have to do for him, because I love my kitten.

Name _____ Date _____

12 The narrator picks Jethro to take home from the farm because Jethro is—

○ the best-behaved of all the kittens

○ the only kitten that has tiger-stripes

○ the biggest of all the kittens

○ the first kitten to come forward

13 In paragraph 5, what does the word <u>snarled</u> mean?

○ Thin

○ Twisted

○ Wet

○ Shiny

14 What happens when it is discovered that Jethro has ear mites?

○ Jethro's eyes are checked.

○ Jethro is put in his carrier.

○ Jethro gets medicine.

○ Jethro's heart is checked.

15 As Jethro gets older, the narrator will most likely—

○ take Jethro back to the farm

○ continue to take care of Jethro

○ stop visiting Jethro on weekends

○ decide to get another kitten like Jethro

16 Which word best describes Grandma in the story?

○ Funny

○ Fair

○ Careful

○ Loving

GO ON

Name _____ Date _____

> # Read the selection. Then read each question that follows it.
> # Decide which is the best answer to each question.
> # Mark the space for the answer you have chosen.

Friends Go Shopping

1   Sonja, Urie, and Gabrielle were shopping with Urie's mom at the mall one day. They always enjoyed each other's company when strolling through the stores and daydreaming about wearing the newest fashions. There was one catch today, though—they only had five dollars each to spend.

2   The girls were eager to take a peek at the jewelry store, the music store, and the many other interesting shops in the mall. They couldn't help dashing across the mall and through the stores. Urie told her friends that she was starting to get hungry. They headed over to the food court, where a variety of snacks were available. Soon most of their money was gone.

3   After lunch, the girls continued shopping. As Sonja passed a clothing store, she stopped suddenly, and Urie and Gabrielle turned to look at Sonja. "What is it, Sonja?" asked Gabrielle.

4   "That sweater in the store window," answered Sonja, "I just have to get it!"

5   "I bet that style would look amazing on you," said Urie, "and it looks like the store carries one in your favorite color!"

6   "I know. I love that shade of purple," said Sonja. "I've been hunting for one just like it for months!" Sonja rushed into the store and tried the sweater on, hoping it would fit. The sweater fit perfectly. But the price was more than Sonja could afford.

7   Sonja remembered shopping with her mother a few months ago. Sonja's mother had wanted to buy a dress that she had tried on. But the store only had one dress in her size, and it had a large smear of dirt on the collar. When Sonja's mother brought the soiled dress to

© Houghton Mifflin Harcourt Publishing Company. All rights reserved.

Name _____ Date _____

the salesclerk's attention, he had given her a discount. Sonja's mother bought the dress at a reduced price, and she had removed the stain at home.

8 In vain Sonja examined the sweater for flaws, but she didn't find any stains or tears. "What if I 'accidentally' got lipstick on this?" Sonja wondered. "Would I get a discount, too? But that would be dishonest," she said to herself, as she reluctantly put the sweater back on the clothing rack and joined her friends.

9 "I need to talk to you two," she said. "I really need your opinion. I want that sweater, but I don't have enough money to buy it." Sonja quickly told her friends about her mother's dress. "I'm tempted to get it dirty and ask for a discount. What do you think?"

10 "Sonja, that's not like you," Gabrielle said, frowning. "Why don't you just wait until you have the money?"

11 "But how would I ever get enough money to buy that sweater?" asked Sonja.

12 "You can do extra chores at home," answered Urie. "If you save all of your money, you'll have enough in no time."

13 Sonja looked at the sweater and then turned back to her friends. "You're right. I can earn the money if I work hard. I'm lucky to have friends who always remind me of the right thing to do!"

© Houghton Mifflin Harcourt Publishing Company. All rights reserved.

Name _____ Date _____

17 The story mostly takes place in a—
- ⬯ food court
- ⬯ music store
- ⬯ clothing store
- ⬯ bookstore

18 Sonja's main problem is that—
- ⬯ her friends want to leave her to go to the food court
- ⬯ she doesn't know which color would look best on her
- ⬯ she doesn't have enough money to buy something
- ⬯ her friends don't like the sweater she likes

19 What is the main lesson Sonja learns in the story?
- ⬯ Making enough money to buy clothes can be difficult.
- ⬯ Having friends who look out for you is important.
- ⬯ Shopping with friends is a lot of fun.
- ⬯ Buying new clothes is expensive.

20 What would most likely have happened if Sonja had made a different decision?
- ⬯ She would feel guilty about her choice.
- ⬯ Her friends would be proud of her.
- ⬯ Her friends would make the same choice.
- ⬯ She would have gotten her friends in trouble.

21 Gabrielle, Sonja, and Urie are alike because they—
- ⬯ save their money to buy new clothes
- ⬯ like the same color
- ⬯ enjoy going shopping
- ⬯ do extra chores to earn money

> **Read the selection. Then read each question that follows it.**
> **Decide which is the best answer to each question.**
> **Mark the space for the answer you have chosen.**

A New Ball Game

1   How are a peach basket and a basketball hoop alike? Read the story. You will find out.

2   A long time ago, there was a gym teacher named Mr. Naismith. He had a hard time keeping his class busy. His students were bored. They talked too loudly. They didn't like to stay inside in winter. Mr. Naismith tried to think of a way to keep his class busy.

3   Mr. Naismith had an idea. He asked someone at the school to find two boxes. No boxes could be found. Mr. Naismith got two peach baskets. He put the peach baskets high above the gym floor. One basket was at one end of the gym. The other basket was at the other end.

4   Mr. Naismith had a surprise for his students the next day. They saw the peach baskets. They thought that was funny. Mr. Naismith told them the rules of his new game. There would be two teams. Each team would try to throw a ball into a peach basket. The teams would not play against each other. They would just try to get a ball into their own basket.

5   There was one main rule. When a player had the ball, he had to pass it to another player. The player who got the ball would throw it into the basket. The students had a hard time passing the ball. Everyone wanted to keep the ball. They wanted to throw it in the basket.

6   The players could not push each other. They also could not hit. If they did, Mr. Naismith would blow his whistle and that team would get a foul. After three fouls, the other team would get a point.

7   When a player threw the ball into the basket, it stayed there! There were no holes in the bottoms of the peach baskets. Mr. Naismith had to climb a ladder to get the ball out of the basket. Then players could shoot the ball again. It was a slow game.

Name _____ Date _____

8   Mr. Naismith thought of some changes. He cut out the bottoms of the baskets. That way Mr. Naismith wouldn't have to climb a ladder to get a ball. The rules of the game changed too. The teams started to play against each other. Then players could bounce the ball. The game wasn't so slow any more.

9   The students loved peach basketball. They asked Mr. Naismith to play the game inside and outside. The students showed their friends how to play. Everyone loved the game. After a while, peach baskets were changed to hoops and nets. Does this sound familiar? Peach baskets became basketball hoops. The game of basketball was invented.

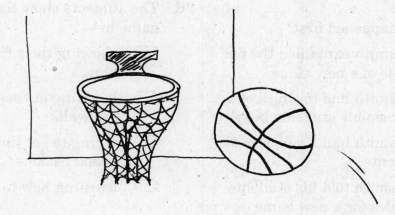

GO ON

© Houghton Mifflin Harcourt Publishing Company. All rights reserved.

22 Which of the following best describes why the author wrote this article?

- ⬭ To inform people of the rules of basketball
- ⬭ To encourage people to play a new kind of game
- ⬭ To show how Mr. Naismith became a popular teacher
- ⬭ To explain how the game of basketball was invented

23 Which event happened first?

- ⬭ Mr. Naismith explained the one main rule of a new game.
- ⬭ Mr. Naismith had to think of a way to keep his students busy.
- ⬭ Mr. Naismith had a surprise for his students.
- ⬭ Mr. Naismith told his students about rules for a new game.

24 The main rule of peach basketball was that players—

- ⬭ were out of the game if they had two fouls
- ⬭ had to pass the ball
- ⬭ had to shoot as soon as they got the ball
- ⬭ were not to bounce the ball

25 How does Mr. Naismith solve the problem of having to get the ball out of the basket?

- ⬭ He lets the students get the ball.
- ⬭ He moves the game outside.
- ⬭ He cuts out the bottoms of the baskets.
- ⬭ He puts the baskets lower on the wall.

26 The students show they love the new game by—

- ⬭ showing their friends how to play
- ⬭ laughing at the peach baskets on the walls
- ⬭ trying to get the ball into the peach baskets
- ⬭ learning how to bounce the ball

27 Which word best describes Mr. Naismith?

- ⬭ Tired
- ⬭ Calm
- ⬭ Clever
- ⬭ Funny

GO ON ➤

> **Read the selection. Then read each question that follows it.**
> **Decide which is the best answer to each question.**
> **Mark the space for the answer you have chosen.**

Lazy Day

by Eileen Spinelli
illustrated by Stephanie Roth

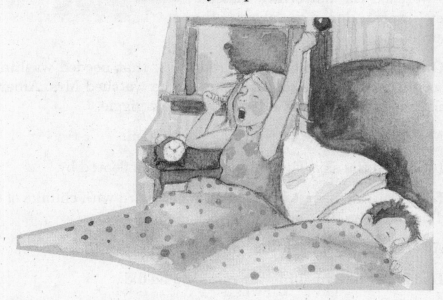

1   One fine day Mama woke up long after the alarm clock went off. "Today is Lazy Day!" she declared.

2   So breakfast was berries and bananas, and nobody cooked.

3   We all left our bowls in the sink and went outside where there was plenty to look at.

4   For the rest of the morning we took it easy and did nothing but look.

GO ON

5   Daddy looked at the shed that needed painting. But nobody paints on Lazy Day. So he watched the squirrels instead. They were scurrying around the yard looking for something good to eat.

6   Grandma looked at the weeds sprouting in her flower garden. But nobody pulls weeds on Lazy Day. So she watched the butterflies instead. They were dancing above the petunias.

7   Grandpa looked at his dusty red truck that needed washing. But nobody washes trucks on Lazy Day. So he watched Mrs. Albert's pet duck chase the mail carrier and got quite a giggle.

8   Mama watched our cat stalking a sunbeam.

9   I watched the sky. Two ship-shaped clouds floated by.

10   Lazy Day lunch was a picnic in the backyard with chunks of cheese and hunks of bread, and nobody cooked.

11   After lunch Mama felt like singing. So she did.

12   Daddy felt like smelling the roses. So he did.

13   Grandma felt like taking a nap.

14   Grandpa felt like taking off his shoes and socks.

15   I felt like splashing in an old garden tub. So I did.

GO ON

16   Dinner on Lazy Day was cold leftovers on paper plates, and nobody cooked.

17   After dinner there was plenty to entertain us. Fireflies and moonrise. Bats against the starlight. Owls hooting. Crickets chirping. Bullfrogs croaking. Neighbors waving and joking about us lazybones lolling in rocking chairs.

18   But that's how it is on Lazy Day. You don't have to do a thing. You just have to be.

28 In paragraph 6, what does the word <u>sprouting</u> mean?

- ⬭ Growing
- ⬭ Wilting
- ⬭ Dying
- ⬭ Planting

29 According to the story, breakfast, lunch, and dinner are alike because all three meals—

- ⬭ are served on paper plates
- ⬭ are berries and bananas
- ⬭ are not cooked
- ⬭ are leftovers

30 Which event takes place last in the story?

- ⬭ Daddy watches squirrels.
- ⬭ Grandma looks at the weeds.
- ⬭ Grandpa takes off his socks.
- ⬭ Grandpa giggles at the duck.

31 What will Daddy most likely do tomorrow?

- ⬭ Declare that it's a Lazy Day
- ⬭ Pull some weeds
- ⬭ Paint the shed
- ⬭ Splash in a tub

32 What was the author's main purpose for writing "Lazy Day"?

- ⬭ To tell interesting facts about holidays
- ⬭ To tell a story about one family's special day
- ⬭ To show people different ways to relax
- ⬭ To give information about different chores

Name _____ Date _____

Writing: Revising and Editing

> **Read the introduction and the passage that follows it. Then read each question. Decide which is the best answer to each question. Mark the space for the answer you have chosen.**

Francisco is a third-grader. He wrote this draft in which he describes an outdoor experience. Read the paper and think about changes that could make the writing better. Then answer the questions that follow.

Telling the Truth

(1) Last spring I visited my cousins, Hilda and Hector, for a week.

(2) They live in denver, Colorado. (3) The first day, they took me

mountain biking. (4) I can ride a regular bike, but I had never ridden a

mountain bike. (5) Hilda let me use her extra mountain bike and helmet.

(6) I practiced riding the bike in my cousins' neighborhood. (7) It was

easy the hard part came later.

(8) We went to a forest that has biking trails through it. (9) I was

enjoying the ride until we came to a steep hill. (10) My legs began to ache

as I pedaled up the hill. (11) We came to a downhill part that scared me.

(12) Somehow, I got down the hill without falling. (13) I wasn't enjoying

© Houghton Mifflin Harcourt Publishing Company. All rights reserved.

mountain biking, but I didn't want to tell my cousins. (14) When the ride

was over that day. (15) I was so glad. (16) I pretended I'd had a great

time, though.

(17) The next day, my cousins said, "Let's ride mountain bikes again!"

(18) I didn't want to say no, but I had to tell them the truth. (19) They

didn't miend at all. (20) We decided to visit the aquarium instead, which

was a lot more fun than mountain biking!

GO ON

© Houghton Mifflin Harcourt Publishing Company. All rights reserved.

Name _____ Date _____

1 What change should be made in sentence 2?

◯ Change *They* to **they**

◯ Change *live* to **lives**

◯ Change *in* to **to**

◯ Change *denver* to **Denver**

2 What is the **BEST** way to revise sentence 7?

◯ It was easy the hard part, came later.

◯ It was easy the hard part. Came later.

◯ It was easy. The hard part came later.

◯ It was easy so the hard part came later.

3 What is the **BEST** way to rewrite sentence 11?

◯ We came to a downhill. Part that scared me.

◯ First, we came to a downhill part that scared me.

◯ Next, we came to a downhill part that scared me.

◯ Today, we came to a downhill part that scared me.

4 What is the **BEST** way to combine sentences 14 and 15?

◯ When the ride over that day I so was glad.

◯ When the ride was over that day, I was so glad.

◯ When the ride was over that day and I was so glad.

◯ When the ride was over that day, but I was so glad.

5 What change, if any, should be made in sentence 19?

◯ Change *They* to **Them**

◯ Change *didn't* to **did'nt**

◯ Change *miend* to **mind**

◯ Make no change

GO ON

© Houghton Mifflin Harcourt Publishing Company. All rights reserved.

Read the introduction and the passage that follows it. Then read each question. Decide which is the best answer to each question. Mark the space for the answer you have chosen.

Hailey is in the third grade. She wrote this report about sleep. This is a draft of Hailey's report. Read the report and think about the changes that could make it better. Then answer the questions that follow.

We All Need Sleep

(1) A good night's sleep is important to our health and learning. (2) Have you noticed how you feel. (3) When you don't get enough sleep? (4) Growing kids need about ten hours of sleep each night.

(5) Animals also need sleep. (6) Octopuses, otters, foxs, and fruit flies all snooze and slumber. (7) Researchers are learning about the sleep

patterns of different animals. (8) Some animals seam to need more sleep than others. (9) For example, an elephant only sleeps for two to four hours a day, but an opossum sleeps for almast twenty hours a day. (10) Some animals, such as horses, sleep standing up. (11) Others, such as bats, sleep upside down.

(12) Some animals are half-awake when they are sleeping. (13) Whales and dolphins keep one eye open and half of their brains awake when they sleep to protect themselves in the Ocean. (14) When ducks sleep in a group, the birds on the outside edge sleep with half their brains awake and their eyes partially open.

(15) Scientists still have a lot to learn about sleep in people and in animals. (16) They know one thing for sure, though. (17) Whether you're a person or a porcupine, you can't live without sleep.

GO ON ➡

6 What is the **BEST** way to combine sentences 2 and 3?

- ⬭ Have you noticed how you feel when you don't get enough sleep?
- ⬭ How you feel have you noticed when you don't get enough sleep?
- ⬭ Have you noticed how when you feel when you don't get enough sleep?
- ⬭ When have you noticed how you feel when you don't get enough sleep?

7 What change, if any, should be made in sentence 6?

- ⬭ Change *Octopuses* to **octopuses**
- ⬭ Changes *foxs* to **foxes**
- ⬭ Insert a period after *snooze*
- ⬭ Make no change

8 What change should be made in sentence 8?

- ⬭ Change *animals* to **animales**
- ⬭ Change *seam* to **seem**
- ⬭ Change *than* to **and**
- ⬭ Change the period to a question mark

9 What change, if any, should be made in sentence 9?

- ⬭ Change *elephant* to **elephants**
- ⬭ Change *two* to **too**
- ⬭ Change *almast* to **almost**
- ⬭ Make no change

10 What change should be made in sentence 13?

- ⬭ Change *Whales* to **Whals**
- ⬭ Change *dolphins* to **Dolphins**
- ⬭ Insert a period after *open*
- ⬭ Change *Ocean* to **ocean**

© Houghton Mifflin Harcourt Publishing Company. All rights reserved.

Writing: Written Composition

> Write a personal narrative in which you describe a personal experience that you will always remember.

Use a separate sheet of paper to plan your composition. Then write your composition on the lined pages that follow.

The information in the box below will help you remember what you should think about when you write your personal narrative.

REMEMBER—YOU SHOULD

❑ write about a personal experience that you will always remember

❑ use a strong beginning to get the reader's attention and tell what your narrative is about

❑ use sensory details that tell how something looked, sounded, smelled, tasted, or felt

❑ use a strong ending that tells how your experience worked out or how you felt

❑ try to use correct spelling, capitalization, punctuation, grammar, and sentences

© Houghton Mifflin Harcourt Publishing Company. All rights reserved.

Name _____ Date _____

_____

_____

_____

_____

_____

_____

_____

_____

_____

_____

_____

_____

_____

_____

_____

© Houghton Mifflin Harcourt Publishing Company. All rights reserved.

Name _____ Date _____

_____

_____

_____

_____

_____

_____

_____

_____

_____

_____

_____

_____

_____

© Houghton Mifflin Harcourt Publishing Company. All rights reserved.

Reading

> **Read the selection. Then read each question that follows it.**
> **Decide which is the best answer to each question.**
> **Mark the space for the answer you have chosen.**

Treasures Found

1   Katie was strolling down the main hall at school. The bell had just rung and signaled the end of another school week. Katie's friend Xavier walked alongside her, telling her about his plans for the weekend. Suddenly Katie stopped listening as a sign on the wall caught her eye. It displayed "ART CONTEST" in large, bold letters across the top. Katie read aloud the information on the sign.

2   *Students in all grades can enter the art contest. Pick up an entry form in the school office, fill it in, and return it to the office by February 6. All artwork is due by March 1. Famous wood <u>carver</u> Antonio Gonzalez will be one of the judges. Contest winners will be <u>announced</u> on March 5.*

3   Katie turned to Xavier and said excitedly, "I'm going to submit something to the contest!" As Katie got on the bus, her head buzzed with ideas. She thought about painting a picture of her dog, Biscuit. Then she thought about making something with clay. There were so many choices!

4   When she got home, Katie continued to <u>imagine</u> ideas for her artwork. She made a few <u>sketches</u> of Biscuit. Katie's younger brother wanted to help her with the artwork. "No, Matt, I have to do this by myself," Katie told him. She could see that Matt was disappointed, so she said, "Let's go play outside!" Matt's face brightened as he ran ahead of her out the door.

5   After playing for some time, the two stopped to wander through their backyard. "Look!" said Matt, "I found a pretty feather!" He picked up the blue feather and showed it to Katie. Then he put it in his pocket and continued to look on the <u>lawn</u>. "I found something else," he called as he ran over to Katie and handed her three white pebbles.

© Houghton Mifflin Harcourt Publishing Company. All rights reserved.

6   Katie was finding interesting things, too. She found some thin, curly twigs and crisp brown leaves. Katie began to picture a design made from the objects they had found. She asked Matt to help her <u>collect</u> more items. After some intense searching, they went back inside.

7   Katie put a sheet of poster board on the kitchen table. Then she and Matt spread out the objects they had found on it. "Watch this," Katie told Matt as she began to arrange the objects, putting items with different textures together. She put the smooth white pebbles next to the crunchy brown leaves. She sprinkled dried grass here and there on the board. Katie studied the arrangement and said, "It needs a few more things."

8   Matt leapt from his chair and declared, "I'll find some more!" He hurried out the back door again. Katie watched as her brother sat on the grass and inspected the ground carefully. Then he moved to another place in the yard. Katie <u>returned</u> to arranging the objects. About 30 minutes later, Matt came back inside. His pockets <u>bulged</u> with the treasures he'd found in the yard.

9   "Let's see what you've found," Katie said. Matt dug into one pocket and produced two old pennies and a snail shell. He reached into the other pocket and pulled out a rock the size of his fist, a snack <u>wrapper</u>, and a walnut shell. "Oh, my!" Katie said. "I really <u>appreciate</u> your hard work, Matt. These are all great things that can be used in the artwork."

10   For the <u>rest</u> of the weekend, Katie worked on her project. She had decided not to paint a picture of Biscuit. Instead, she found an old drawer in the garage that her dad said she could have. Katie painted it green and blue and glued the other objects to its inside.

11   Katie named the artwork "Found Treasures" and entered it in the contest. She did not win the art contest, but she was only a little disappointed. The judges gave her an "honorable mention" ribbon, which meant that her artwork was good enough to be recognized as special. Katie knew that Matt would be excited about the ribbon. She could hardly wait to get home that day to give it to him.

1   At the beginning of the story, why does Katie stop listening to Xavier?

   ◯   She is late for the school bus.

   ◯   She is thinking about her artwork.

   ◯   She is bored by what Xavier says.

   ◯   She sees the sign for the art contest.

2   In paragraph 2, what does the word carver mean?

   ◯   A type of artist

   ◯   A form to fill out

   ◯   A place where a contest is held

   ◯   A person who judges a contest

3   Right after Katie sees the sign, she decides to—

   ◯   play with her dog

   ◯   enter the art contest

   ◯   find objects outdoors

   ◯   take a walk with Matt

4   What does the word imagine mean in paragraph 4?

   ◯   Ignore

   ◯   Think about

   ◯   Shout

   ◯   Turn away

5   In paragraph 4, the word sketches means—

   ◯   drawings

   ◯   ideas

   ◯   stories

   ◯   papers

6   From the story, the reader can tell that—

   ◯   Katie is a good student

   ◯   Xavier lives near Katie

   ◯   Katie enjoys making art

   ◯   Matt does not like to go outside

7   In paragraph 6, the word collect means—

   ◯   find

   ◯   study

   ◯   gather

   ◯   form

8   How does Matt probably feel when Katie uses his objects in her artwork?

   ◯   Unlucky

   ◯   Pleased

   ◯   Angry

   ◯   Sad

GO ON ➡

9 What happens right after Katie says the artwork needs a few more things?

◯ Matt finds a blue feather.

◯ Katie and Matt go for a walk.

◯ Katie enters the artwork in the contest.

◯ Matt goes outside to look for more objects.

10 What does the word <u>bulged</u> mean in paragraph 8?

◯ Looked odd

◯ Ripped apart

◯ Were open

◯ Were full

11 Read the meanings below for the word <u>appreciate</u>.

---

ap•pre•ci•ate (ə-'prē-shē-āt) *verb*

1. to be grateful

2. to understand

3. to recognize

4. to grow in number

Which meaning best fits the way <u>appreciate</u> is used in paragraph 9?

◯ Meaning 1

◯ Meaning 2

◯ Meaning 3

◯ Meaning 4

12 In paragraph 10, the word <u>rest</u> means—

◯ to relax

◯ a quiet time

◯ to stay in place

◯ the remaining part

13 Why does Katie decide not to paint a picture of Biscuit?

◯ She is not pleased with her painting.

◯ Biscuit will not sit still for a painting.

◯ She discovers another way to make artwork.

◯ Matt asks her to use found objects to make artwork.

14 What does Katie do before she glues the objects in the drawer?

◯ She creates a title for the artwork.

◯ She gets a ribbon from the judges.

◯ She enters the artwork in the contest.

◯ She paints the drawer green and blue.

GO ON ➤

15 Which word has the same sound
as the underlined part of the word
ann<u>ou</u>nced?

○ Through

○ Smooth

○ Brown

○ Could

16 Which word has the same sound as
the underlined part of the word l<u>aw</u>n?

○ Cross

○ Down

○ Latch

○ Nail

17 Which of these shows the correct way
to divide the word <u>returned</u>?

○ retur • ned

○ re • turned

○ r • eturned

○ ret • urned

18 Which word has the same sound
as the underlined part of the word
<u>wr</u>apper?

○ when

○ ring

○ well

○ light

GO ON

Name _____ Date _____

Read the selection. Then read each question that follows it.
Decide which is the best answer to each question.
Mark the space for the answer you have chosen.

Pine Elementary School Science Fair

PINE ELEMENTARY SCHOOL PRESENTS
Student Science Fair
For Students in Grades K–5
Dates: October 30–31
Location: Pine Elementary School Gym

Explore Your World . . . Think Like a Scientist

1 The Student Science Fair offers a great way for you to put your science knowledge to use! Whether or not you win, you'll have fun at this contest.

Science Fair Events

2 There is plenty to do during the science fair. Of course, you'll want to take a look at all of the students' projects. There will be other exciting things to see and do as well. These events will highlight the wonderful world of science. The big event is the announcement of the winners in each

grade. This announcement will take place at the <u>awards</u> ceremony on Friday afternoon. Many of the other events are listed below.

© Houghton Mifflin Harcourt Publishing Company. All rights reserved.

Name _____ Date _____

Meet a Robot!

3   Can people and robots work together? Learn <u>about</u> the latest <u>research</u> being done to make that happen. Scientists will be at the fair on Thursday, October 30, with Modo. What's Modo? It is a robot helper being developed to help people with jobs they do. Learn how Modo's large blue eyes are able to "see." Watch Modo grasp objects and wiggle them to get a feel for their size. Then see how Modo places the objects on a shelf. Touch Modo on the arm. Watch what happens! It will respond to your touch. If you push it too hard, it will say, "Ouch!"

4   Modo's visit is a <u>rare</u> public appearance, since the robot does not often leave the <u>laboratory</u>. Be sure to see this amazing robot while you have the chance!

More Robots!

5   The fair will also have other types of robots. They will range from simple ones to more complicated machines. Scientists who built the robots will be at the science fair to show what their inventions can do. They will explain how a robot is "born." The scientists will also answer questions about the design and building of the robots.

Our Own Thomas Edison

6   Make sure you're in the gym at 10:00 A.M. on Friday. That's when local <u>genius</u> Ray Allen will give a talk about his life as an <u>inventor</u>. He will also show some of his early gadgets. At the end of his talk, Mr. Allen will take questions from the <u>audience</u>.

SCIENCE FAIR SCHEDULE

7

Registration
  October 27 7:30 A.M.–5:00 P.M.

Set-up of Projects
  October 28 10:00 A.M.–3:00 P.M.
  October 29 10:00 A.M.–3:00 P.M.

Science Fair Viewing
  October 30 10:00 A.M.–3:00 P.M.
  October 31 10:00 A.M.–3:00 P.M.

Awards Presentation
  October 31 1:00 P.M.

© Houghton Mifflin Harcourt Publishing Company. All rights reserved.

HOW TO SIGN UP

8   Get a sign-up form in the Pine Elementary School office. Complete the form and turn it in by 5:00 P.M. on Monday, October 27. You will also receive a science fair booklet. The booklet will give you suggestions on how to choose a topic for a science fair project and how to create a display. It will also list sources of ideas for projects. Information on what you must include in a display can be found in the booklet.

WHY TAKE PART IN THE SCIENCE FAIR?

9   *You can*

- explore the world of science in a project of your choice
- share your knowledge and interests with others
- meet scientists and get their advice
- view your classmates' thrilling science projects
- see who wins the science prize

This is last year's winner!

WHO ARE THE JUDGES?

10   The Pine Elementary School Science Committee will choose the judges, which will include science teachers and local scientists.

Contact Information

If you have any questions, contact Jenny McAllister at 555-1845 or Wynn Adams at 555-2331.

GO ON

Look at the chart and use it to answer the question below.

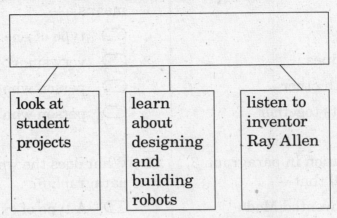

19 Which of the following belongs in the empty box?
- ⬭ A School Science Fair
- ⬭ A Public Appearance
- ⬭ An Awards Ceremony
- ⬭ A Schedule of Events

20 The boxed words belong to the same category.

fair, ceremony, contest

Which word names the category?
- ⬭ Projects
- ⬭ Events
- ⬭ Announcements
- ⬭ Objects

21 In paragraph 2, which word means almost the same as the word <u>awards</u>?
- ⬭ Activities
- ⬭ Winners
- ⬭ Prizes
- ⬭ Projects

GO ON ▶

© Houghton Mifflin Harcourt Publishing Company. All rights reserved.

Name _____ Date _____

22 In paragraph 3, the word <u>research</u> means—

- ⬭ fact finding
- ⬭ using machines
- ⬭ working with others
- ⬭ putting parts together

23 From the information in paragraph 3, the reader can tell that—

- ⬭ Ray Allen invented Modo
- ⬭ Modo falls over easily
- ⬭ Scientists are still developing Modo
- ⬭ Modo robots will be for sale

24 In paragraph 4, the word <u>rare</u> means—

- ⬭ fine
- ⬭ thin
- ⬭ unusual
- ⬭ nearly raw

25 What does the word <u>laboratory</u> mean in paragraph 4?

- ⬭ The place where a scientist lives
- ⬭ The place where a scientist works
- ⬭ A place where a science fair is held
- ⬭ A place where students learn about science

26 In paragraph 6, the word <u>genius</u> means a—

- ⬭ type of scientist
- ⬭ very smart person
- ⬭ person who is famous
- ⬭ person who gives speeches

27 What does the word <u>inventor</u> mean in paragraph 6?

- ⬭ A type of experiment
- ⬭ A type of science project
- ⬭ A person who enjoys science
- ⬭ A person who creates something

28 Why will many students be in the gym at 1:00 P.M. on Friday?

- ⬭ Modo will appear.
- ⬭ Registration takes place.
- ⬭ The awards will be announced.
- ⬭ Ray Allen will give an interview.

29 Students can get sign-up forms for the science fair in the—

- ⬭ gym
- ⬭ office
- ⬭ library
- ⬭ cafeteria

GO ON ➡

© Houghton Mifflin Harcourt Publishing Company. All rights reserved.

30 According to the information in paragraph 9, students who take part in the fair can—

- ⬭ design a robot
- ⬭ meet scientists
- ⬭ judge a contest
- ⬭ become scientists

31 The pictures in the brochure help the reader understand that—

- ⬭ most schools have science fairs
- ⬭ there will be a robot at the science fair
- ⬭ a famous scientist will be at the science fair
- ⬭ students should build a robot for the science fair

32 The headings in dark type help the reader—

- ⬭ understand the pictures in the brochure
- ⬭ learn important dates in the science fair
- ⬭ find important information about the fair
- ⬭ find phone numbers for contact information

33 Which word has the same sound as the underlined part of the word ab<u>out</u>?

- ⬭ Look
- ⬭ Show
- ⬭ World
- ⬭ Crowd

34 Which word has the same sound as the underlined part of the word <u>au</u>dience?

- ⬭ Walk
- ⬭ Range
- ⬭ Class
- ⬭ Share

35 Which word means about the same thing as the word <u>thrilling</u>?

- ⬭ Working
- ⬭ Winning
- ⬭ Exciting
- ⬭ Expecting

© Houghton Mifflin Harcourt Publishing Company. All rights reserved.

Writing: Revising and Editing

> **Read the introduction and the passage that follows it. Then read each question. Decide which is the best answer to each question. Mark the space for the answer you have chosen.**

Elliot is a third grade student. He wrote this story about a special gift that he received. Read Elliot's story and think about ways to help him correct and improve the writing. Then answer the questions that follow.

Birthday Chickens

(1) Some receive toys and games for their birthdays, while others receive decorated cards. (2) Last year, I got chickens for this special day. (3) That was the most thoughtful present ever, because I have wanted to raise chickens ever since my family and I moved to the country. (4) Our neighbor has plenty of livestock, including chickens, and our neighbor would let me help collect eggs. (5) I enjoyed watching the rooster and hens scratch around in her yard, pecking the ground for food. (6) I know it sounds silly, but I just loved those chickens and wanted some of my very own.

(7) First, I went to the library and checked out books about chickens. (8) Next, I asked Mom and Dad to let me raise chickens. (9) I told them that I had read everything I could find about raising and taking care of

GO ON

chickens. (10) They wanted to make sure I was really going to look after them. (11) I promised that I would and reminded them that we would also have free eggs! (12) Then Mom built a coop. (13) Dad built a coop. (14) I built a coop next to our barn. (15) We also built a fence around the coop so the chickens would have a place to roam and peck.

(16) On my birthday, I came home from school, not expecting anything special. (17) Guess what was in the coop? (18) There were four beautiful and fluffy little baby chicks! (19) That's much better than a toy or a game. (20) A toy or a game is not as good.

GO ON

1 What is the **BEST** way to revise sentence 1?

◯ Change *birthdays* to **Birthdays**

◯ Add **people** after *Some*

◯ Add **people** after *others*

◯ Change the comma to a period

2 What is the **BEST** way to revise sentence 4?

◯ Our neighbor has plenty of livestock, including chickens, and she would let me help collect eggs.

◯ Our neighbor has plenty of livestock, including chickens. Our neighbor would let me help collect eggs.

◯ Our neighbor have plenty of livestock, including chickens, and our neighbor would let me help collect eggs.

◯ Our neighbor she has livestock and chickens, and our neighbor would let me help collect eggs.

3 Which sentence could **BEST** be added before sentence 7?

◯ I wanted my own chickens more than anything else.

◯ My neighbor has several chickens.

◯ I prepared a plan that was guaranteed to work.

◯ I asked Mom and Dad if I could have chickens.

4 What is the **BEST** way to combine sentences 12, 13, and 14?

◯ Then Mom Dad and I built a coop next to our barn.

◯ Then Mom Dad, and I built a coop next to our barn.

◯ Then Mom, Dad, and I built a coop next to our barn.

◯ Then Mom built a coop, Dad and I built a coop next to our barn.

5 Which sentence does **NOT** belong in this paper?

◯ Sentence 3

◯ Sentence 5

◯ Sentence 11

◯ Sentence 20

GO ON ➡

> # Read the introduction and the passage that follows it. Then read each question. Decide which is the best answer to each question. Mark the space for the answer you have chosen.

Tanya is in the third grade. Her teacher asked each student to write about a type of bird. Tanya wrote about the bald eagle. Read the draft of her paper and think about changes that could make it better. Then answer the questions that follow.

Our National Bird

(1) Can you name the national bird of the United States? (2) It's the

bald eagle. (3) Of course, the bald eagle's rownd head is not really bald.

(4) Its name comes from the Old English word balde, which means "white."

(5) Both the heads and tails of bald eagles are white.

(6) Female bald eagles are typically larger than male bald eagles.

(7) The wings of a female bald eagle stretch about 8 feet from wing tip to wing tip. (8) That length is about the distance from the floor to the ceiling of most rooms!

(9) Bald eagles' nests are larger than any other bird in North America. (10) Female bald eagles build their nests at the top of tall trees in order to protect their eggs. (11) Baby eagles are light gray when they are born. (12) Later, they turn brown and white.

(13) In fact, they can fly to heights of up to 10,000 feet. (14) They swoop down from above and animals such as fish. (15) An eagle glides over the water, grabs a fish with its feet, and flies away to eat it.

(16) Bald eagles can live for 30 years or more. (17) They are once almost extinct, or completely destroyed, because of pollution and hunting. (18) Bald eagles are no longer in danger of extinction because of laws passed to protect bald eagles.

6 What change, if any, should be made in sentence 3?

- ⬭ Change *rownd* to **round**
- ⬭ Change *bald* to **bold**
- ⬭ Change the comma to a period
- ⬭ Make no change

7 Which sentence could **BEST** be added before sentence 13?

- ⬭ Bald eagles are proud birds.
- ⬭ Bald eagles have white heads.
- ⬭ Bald eagles are masters of the sky.
- ⬭ Bald eagles are no longer in danger.

8 What is the **BEST** way to revise sentence 14?

- ⬭ Change *swoop* to **swooping**
- ⬭ Add **catch** after *and*
- ⬭ Add a period after *animals*
- ⬭ Change *fish* to **Fish**

9 Which change, if any, should be made in sentence 17?

- ⬭ Change *are* to **were**
- ⬭ Add a comma after *once*
- ⬭ Change *They* to **Them**
- ⬭ Add a comma after *pollution*

10 What is the **BEST** way to revise sentence 18?

- ⬭ Bald eagles are no longer in danger, laws passed to protect them from extinction.
- ⬭ Bald eagles are no longer in danger of extinction because of laws passed to protect them.
- ⬭ Bald eagles are no longer in danger because of the laws of extinction passed to protect bald eagles.
- ⬭ Because of laws passed to protect bald eagles are no longer in danger of extinction because of them.

Writing: Written Composition

> ## Read the story below and respond to the prompt that follows it.

A Visit with Aunt Liza

As Andy sat on a rock near the park entrance, he stared at the group of people gathered around his Aunt Liza. It was the first time that Andy had seen his Aunt Liza at work as a park ranger.

"That's the end of the tour," Aunt Liza told the group of park visitors. "I hope you enjoyed learning about the park and its animals."

The crowd clapped and thanked Aunt Liza for sharing so much information about the park and its history. Aunt Liza answered a few more questions and then walked over to Andy. "Are you ready for your personal tour of the park?" Aunt Liza asked him.

Andy slowly nodded his head and looked around him carefully. He had been excited about this visit with his aunt, but he was anxious about the possible dangers in the woods. Andy lived in the city where he was used to seeing animals like squirrels and raccoons, not snakes and bears.

"Stand up," Aunt Liza encouraged, "and let's get going."

Andy got up and started walking next to Aunt Liza. Heading down the trail and glancing at his feet, Andy asked, "What about the snakes?"

"We won't bother the snakes," answered Aunt Liza, patting Andy on the back to try and comfort him.

"You can count on that," Andy muttered. He felt like a fish out of water as he jumped at the sound of leaves crackling under his feet. Andy missed the city's busy sidewalks, familiar smells, and the clean, shiny floors in the apartment building where his family lived.

Aunt Liza pointed at something in a tree down the trail as a blue wing flashed and swooped away.

"Mountain bluebird . . . " Aunt Liza noted as her voice trailed off.

Andy looked at his aunt and noticed she stood speechless and frozen in place.

"What's wrong?" Andy asked as he followed the direction of Aunt Liza's stare. Then he saw it—a bear, and it was looking at them.

Aunt Liza said softly, "It's okay, Andy. This bear seems to sense that we aren't a danger to her. Let's slowly walk back the way we came."

Andy was shaking like a leaf as he began walking backwards up the trail, but he was relieved to see that the bear did not follow them. Back at the park entrance, Andy asked Aunt Liza, "Were you scared?"

"Yes, I was," answered Aunt Liza.

"Why do you like the mountains when there are bears, snakes, and other animals that can hurt you?" asked Andy.

Aunt Liza said, "The mountains are my home. I'm a part of this area, the same as the bears and snakes."

"The same way that I'm a part of the city," Andy said.

Aunt Liza nodded and smiled, "Just like that, Andy."

"I think I'll stay in the city," Andy said with a nervous laugh.

Changing the subject, Aunt Liza smiled as she said, "I'm as hungry as a bear. Why don't we go get something to eat?"

> Do you think Andy should change his mind about liking mountain areas? Write a response that tells why or why not.

Use a separate sheet of paper to plan your composition. Then write your composition on the lined pages that follow.

The information in the box below will help you remember what you should think about when you write your composition.

REMEMBER—YOU SHOULD

❑ write a composition that tells whether or not you think Andy should change his mind

❑ write a strong opening that clearly states your opinion

❑ use a topic sentence to introduce each new reason or idea and support it with details and examples

❑ sum up the reasons for your opinion at the end of your composition

❑ try to use correct spelling, capitalization, punctuation, grammar, and sentences

Name _____ Date _____

_____

_____

_____

_____

_____

_____

_____

_____

_____

_____

_____

_____

_____

_____

_____

_____

_____

© Houghton Mifflin Harcourt Publishing Company. All rights reserved.

Name _____ Date _____

_____

_____

_____

_____

_____

_____

_____

_____

_____

_____

_____

_____

_____

_____

_____

© Houghton Mifflin Harcourt Publishing Company. All rights reserved.

Reading

Read the selection. Then read each question that follows it.
Decide which is the best answer to each question.
Mark the space for the answer you have chosen.

An African Folktale

retold by Marilyn Helmer
illustrated by Josée Masse

1   One day, a farmer decided to dig up some yams to sell at the marketplace. As he worked, he sang:

Sweet, sweet yam, so fine,

Sweet, sweet yam, all mine!

2   He had just pulled the first yam from the earth when it called out to him. "All yours? What are you talking about? Where were you when it was time to weed me and water me?"

3   The farmer was so scared that he jumped to his feet and raced off down the road. By the river, he passed a fisherman with a large fish in his net.

4   "Why are you running so hard on such a hot day?" asked the fisherman.

5   "My yam talked to me!" said the frightened farmer.

6   The fisherman rolled his eyes. "I've never heard of anything so ridiculous," he said.

7   "I agree," said the fish. "Everyone knows that yams can't talk."

8   The fisherman was so surprised that he threw the fish back into the river. Then he scrambled to his feet and ran on down the road, right on the farmer's heels.

9   As the farmer and the fisherman rounded a bend, they came upon a girl carrying a large melon.

10   "Why are you running so fast on such a hot day?" asked the girl.

11   "My yam talked to me!" exclaimed the farmer.

12   "My fish spoke, too!" said the fisherman.

13   The girl laughed so hard she almost dropped her melon. "I've never heard of anything so ridiculous!" she said.

14   "I agree," said the melon. "Everyone knows that yams can't talk."

15   The girl was so terrified that she actually *did* drop the melon. Then she ran away with the farmer and the fisherman as fast as her legs could carry her.

16   Up hill and down, they ran until they came to the King's hut.

17   The farmer stopped to catch his breath. "We must tell the King what is going on," he said.

18   "Yes," said the fisherman, puffing and panting. "The King is a wise man."

19   "He will know exactly what to do," said the girl.

GO ON

© Houghton Mifflin Harcourt Publishing Company. All rights reserved.

20   The three rushed into the King's hut.

21   "My yam talked to me!" said the farmer.

22   The King gave the farmer a <u>stern</u> look. "Impossible," he said. "You have been working too long in the hot sun."

23   "My fish talked to me, too!" said the fisherman.

24   The King frowned. "Nonsense!" he exclaimed. "Your ears are playing tricks on you."

25   "And my melon talked to me!" the girl finally added.

26   The King became very angry. "Foolish tales like that could frighten the entire village," he roared. "Leave my hut immediately before I punish all of you severely!"

27   The farmer, the fisherman and the girl wasted no time in leaving the king's hut. Foolish or not, they did not want to be punished.

28   The King sat back in his royal chair. He shook his head. "Thank goodness they are gone," he muttered to himself. "A talking yam indeed. I've never heard of anything so ridiculous."

29   "I agree," said his chair. "Everyone knows that yams can't talk!"

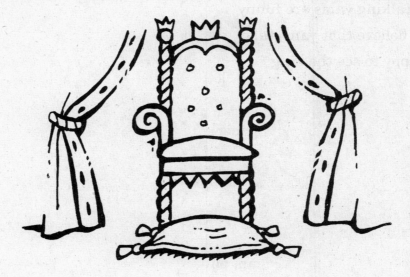

1 In paragraph 22, what does the word
<u>stern</u> mean?

- ⬭ Stare
- ⬭ Serious
- ⬭ Beam
- ⬭ Pleased

2 Which word best describes the
fisherman when the farmer tells him
about the yam?

- ⬭ Scared
- ⬭ Amused
- ⬭ Sad
- ⬭ Happy

3 The farmer, fisherman, and girl are
alike because they all—

- ⬭ run when objects talk
- ⬭ think talking yams are funny
- ⬭ do not believe that yams talk
- ⬭ are happy to see the king

4 What do the farmer, fisherman, and
girl do about the talking objects?

- ⬭ They decide that it is not true.
- ⬭ They dive into the river.
- ⬭ They try to figure out why.
- ⬭ They go to see the king.

5 What happens last in the story?

- ⬭ The fisherman throws the fish in
  the water.
- ⬭ The farmer runs down the road.
- ⬭ The girl drops her melon.
- ⬭ The girl leaves the king's hut.

GO ON ▶

Read the selection. Then read each question that follows it.
Decide which is the best answer to each question.
Mark the space for the answer you have chosen.

The Truth about Bears

1   Three kinds of bears live in the United States. They are the black bear, the brown bear, and the polar bear.

Black Bears

2   Black bears are the most common of the three. They live in forests in many different parts of the country. Even though they are known as "black bears," they are not always black. Sometimes they are brown or tan, and a few are even white. Black bears are usually about five or six feet long, and they are the smallest of the three kinds of bears.

Brown Bears

3   Brown bears are found in a few western states and in Alaska. They live in forests as well as in open areas called the tundra. Brown bears are usually light or dark brown and can grow to be very large. In fact, some are eight feet long!

Polar Bears

4   Polar bears can be found in Alaska, which is in a cold region near the North Pole called the Arctic, where there are no trees. Polar bears are white, and they are the largest of the three kinds of bears. They are a little longer and usually heavier than the brown bear.

Other Interesting Things

5   Bears eat different things. Black and brown bears eat fish and other kinds of meat, roots, and berries. Polar bears eat fish, other meat, seaweed, and grass. All three types of bears eat as much food as they can find just before winter. Then during the cold months they sleep in caves or hollowed out trees called "dens," which keep them warm. Winter is when the female bears have their babies. All three types of bears have between one and four cubs. The cubs are born while the mother bear sleeps!

GO ON

© Houghton Mifflin Harcourt Publishing Company. All rights reserved.

Name _____   Date _____

6   All people are afraid of bears. However, bears are actually shy. Most bears try to stay away from people, but still, bears can be dangerous at times. Mother bears do not want people to get too close to their babies, and bears do not want people to get close to their food!

6 The author wrote this article mainly to—

○ explain why bears sleep all winter

○ describe three kinds of bears

○ tell people not to feed bears

○ show how dangerous bears are

7 Polar bears live—

○ near large forests

○ near the North Pole

○ in many parts of the country

○ in a few western states

8 Why do bears most likely eat as much as they can before winter?

○ They are only hungry just before winter.

○ They are too shy to come out during winter.

○ They cannot find anything to eat in the winter.

○ They sleep all winter and need the nutrition.

9 Which section of the article tells the reader which kind of bear is most common?

○ Black Bears

○ Brown Bears

○ Polar Bears

○ Other Interesting Things

10 Which sentence from the article is an opinion?

○ *Three kinds of bears live in the United States.*

○ *Brown bears are found in a few western states and in Alaska.*

○ *Bears eat different things.*

○ *All people are afraid of bears.*

GO ON ▶

© Houghton Mifflin Harcourt Publishing Company. All rights reserved.

Read the selection. Then read each question that follows it.
Decide which is the best answer to each question.
Mark the space for the answer you have chosen.

Strange Rain

1   Sedat sat on the edge of his bed looking out the window after the thunder had awakened him. He wasn't bothered much because he loved to watch storms. It was so dark and shadowy outside, though, that he could barely see out his window. As the storm continued, he heard an odd, thumping sound followed by what sounded like a bark. Then there was another thumping noise and what sounded like a meow. He decided to reach under his bed for his flashlight.

2   Sedat flipped the switch on the flashlight and pointed it toward the yard. All he could see was the glare from his window. He slipped out of his bed and opened the window and then heard more strange sounds. When he pointed his flashlight into the yard, he could not believe his eyes. It was raining cats and dogs!

3   Sedat rubbed his eyes and looked again. A cat landed softly on its feet and ran under a bush. A dog landed close by, and the cat jumped out. Then the two animals started to play.

4   Sedat saw his cat, Link, walking through the garden. Other cats and dogs rained down in the yard. Sedat worried that Link would disappear into the night with all of the other animals, so he put on his slippers and hurried down the stairs. He opened the back door and called out to Link and noticed that it was barely raining now. As he peered out at the darkness, he saw a cat moving toward him. He called Link's name again, and suddenly, Link ran inside and rubbed against Sedat's legs. Sedat dried Link gently with a towel, carried him upstairs, and fell asleep with his cat curled at the foot of the bed.

© Houghton Mifflin Harcourt Publishing Company. All rights reserved.

5   Sedat woke up early the next morning, and the sun was shining brightly. He dressed quickly and walked downstairs. His mother was opening the back door to go outside, and Sedat went out with her.

6   Sedat's mom looked at the garden. She propped up a flower pot that had been knocked over. Then she cut off a broken branch on another plant.

7   "Look how many plants were damaged during last night's storm," she said. "It must have rained cats and dogs."

8   "Yes, it did," Sedat agreed. He smiled as Link rubbed against his legs and purred.

---

11 The story takes place—
- ○ in a garden
- ○ at Sedat's house
- ○ in Sedat's dream
- ○ in a basement

12 Sedat grabs his flashlight to—
- ○ find Link
- ○ see his mother
- ○ see what is in the yard
- ○ look at the flower pot

13 What does Sedat do to show he cares for Link?
- ○ He watches his cat in the yard.
- ○ Sedat watches Link lick his paws.
- ○ He looks out his window.
- ○ Sedat dries Link with a towel.

14 Which word best describes Sedat?
- ○ Curious
- ○ Funny
- ○ Troubled
- ○ Fearful

15 Which of the following events takes place last in the story?
- ○ Sedat sees a glare from his window.
- ○ Sedat and Link fall asleep.
- ○ Sedat hears a thumping sound.
- ○ Sedat sees it raining cats and dogs.

16 Sedat smiles at the end of the story because—
- ○ Link is safe inside the house
- ○ his mother's garden is unharmed
- ○ his mother goes outside with him
- ○ he knows it rained cats and dogs

GO ON ▶

© Houghton Mifflin Harcourt Publishing Company. All rights reserved.

Name _____ Date _____

**Read the selection. Then read each question that follows it.
Decide which is the best answer to each question.
Mark the space for the answer you have chosen.**

Day and Night in the Desert

art by Paige Billin-Frye

Saguaro cactus blossoms last only one day in the hot desert sun.

1   In late spring, the desert is very hot and dry. But it is full of life. During the cool night, a beautiful saguaro cactus flower blossoms. In the morning, painted lady butterflies suck <u>nectar</u> from wildflowers growing in the sun.

GO ON

© Houghton Mifflin Harcourt Publishing Company. All rights reserved.

Name _____ Date _____

2   Nearby, a hungry lizard watches. It soon <u>snaps</u> up a butterfly and scurries away. Then it rests on a rock warmed by the sun. Lizards have to eat, too.

3   A young snake slithers by, very quietly. It strikes quickly and gobbles up the lizard. The snake won't be hungry for the rest of the day.

This western whiptail lizard has long claws to dig for food and catch insects.

4   Most desert animals stay hidden in the shade during the hot afternoon. But at sunset the desert begins to cool. A roadrunner darts out from behind a barrel cactus. Roadrunners are very quick. The snake is a nice treat.

Roadrunners can't fly very well, so they run fast instead.

5   In the evening, a coyote waits in the darkness. It has begun its night of hunting to bring food to its family. It doesn't bother to chase the roadrunner. A roadrunner is very hard to catch. The coyote looks for a kangaroo rat instead.

GO ON ➡

© Houghton Mifflin Harcourt Publishing Company. All rights reserved.

6   Under the desert moon, another saguaro flower blossoms. In the morning, a butterfly will sip nectar from wildflowers, and the search for food in the desert will begin again.

---

17 What is the article mainly about?
- ⬭ Cactus flowers blooming at night
- ⬭ What desert animals eat
- ⬭ How plants and animals live in the desert
- ⬭ How fast roadrunners can run

18 In paragraph 1, what does <u>nectar</u> mean?
- ⬭ Butterfly food
- ⬭ A type of fruit
- ⬭ A type of plant
- ⬭ Butterfly shelter

19 The desert is hottest—
- ⬭ at sunrise
- ⬭ early in the morning
- ⬭ in the afternoon
- ⬭ at sunset

20 In paragraph 2, what does <u>snaps</u> mean?
- ⬭ Breaks
- ⬭ Catches
- ⬭ Passes
- ⬭ Raises

21 Most desert animals stay hidden in the afternoon to—
- ⬭ sleep
- ⬭ stay cool
- ⬭ eat their prey
- ⬭ hide from enemies

22 According to the article, tomorrow in the desert—
- ⬭ will be very different
- ⬭ the animals will not find food
- ⬭ the same things will happen
- ⬭ the coyote will chase the roadrunner

GO ON ➤

Read the selection. Then read each question that follows it.
Decide which is the best answer to each question.
Mark the space for the answer you have chosen.

Hidden Oak
Elementary School News

Science Section
Mrs. Torres's Science Class Finds Fossils

by: Amy Chang, Grade 3

1   Mrs. Torres is teaching about fossils. They are stone remains of plants and animals. Mrs. Torres wanted to take her class to look for them.

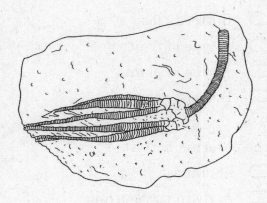

The Trip to Hogtown Creek

2   In December, the class went to a nearby creek. The students started to look for shark teeth. They found many interesting things.

First Fossil

3   Jim Angelo was the first to find something. Jim showed it to Mrs. Torres. She brought all of the students together to see what Jim found. It looked like part of a sand dollar on a rock.

4   Mrs. Torres said it had lived at the bottom of the sea. The stone may become Florida's state fossil. All of the students were excited about that.

More Fossils

5   Jessica Mendez found a shark's tooth. It was very dirty! Mrs. Torres washed it off. Jessica's brother Billy also found a tooth. Mrs. Torres took the finds back to school.

Name _____ Date _____

What We Learned

6   It was a great day at Hogtown Creek. Students looked for fossils, but they are hard to find. It takes time to look for something so old and hidden.

7   The fossils are in Mrs. Torres' classroom. They have been cleaned. Please come to her room to see them.

---

23 The class looks for fossils—

  ◯ in Mrs. Torres' classroom

  ◯ in a creek

  ◯ on the school playground

  ◯ at a beach

24 The first person to discover a fossil at the creek was—

  ◯ Mrs. Torres

  ◯ Amy Chang

  ◯ Jim Angelo

  ◯ Jessica Mendez

25 Which section of the article tells when the class trip occurs?

  ◯ The Trip to Hogtown Creek

  ◯ First Fossil

  ◯ More Fossils

  ◯ What We Learned

26 Amy Chang most likely wrote the article to—

  ◯ describe a trip to look for fossils

  ◯ give information about kinds of fossils

  ◯ show how easy it is to find fossils

  ◯ explain what a sand dollar is

27 If the students return to Hogtown Creek, they most likely will—

  ◯ look for more fossils

  ◯ bring the fossils with them

  ◯ learn about shark teeth

  ◯ study sand dollars

© Houghton Mifflin Harcourt Publishing Company. All rights reserved.

> **Read the selection. Then read each question that follows it.
> Decide which is the best answer to each question.
> Mark the space for the answer you have chosen.**

The Ferris Wheel

1   Have you ever gone on a Ferris wheel high above the city? Do you know who invented this giant wheel that goes round and round? It is an interesting story of a man with big ideas.

2   In 1892, George Ferris talked with the group of people who would build the World's Fair in Chicago. He showed them drawings of a giant wheel between two towers. The wheel looked like two bicycle wheels, but it was 26 stories high! That's as high as some tall city buildings.

3   Mr. Ferris told the group that the wheel would have thirty-six wooden cars on it, and each car would have forty chairs. People would sit in the chairs and ride while the wheel went around.

4   The members of the World's Fair group were uncertain about the wheel; it did not look safe for people, but Mr. Ferris assured them that he would not put people in danger. He was a bridge builder. He knew how to build safe bridges, and he knew how to make the wheel safe. The group consented to allow George Ferris to build his wheel for the fair.

5   Opening day of the Chicago World's Fair was in 1893. People who arrived were surprised to see the huge, tall wheel. The president of the fair shouted, "Ladies and gentlemen, meet Mr. George Ferris. He has invented this new ride. We call it the Ferris Wheel." Then Mr. Ferris, his wife, the mayor of Chicago, and many other people <u>boarded</u> the wheel. They rode up above the city as the wheel turned. The view of the city was spectacular.

6   Everyone wanted to go on the new ride. It was a huge success. Mr. Ferris's big idea is still around. Ferris wheels today look very different from the first Ferris wheel, but the ride is still as much fun.

7   People from all over the world came to the Chicago World's Fair. Look at the chart to learn how long it would have taken visitors to get to Chicago.

Travel Times to Chicago in 1893

From	Estimated Travel Time
Berlin, Germany	11 days
Boston, Massachusetts	32 hours
Edinburgh, Scotland	10 days
London, England	9-1/2 days
Mexico City, Mexico	5 days
Montreal, Quebec, Canada	29 hours
New Orleans, Louisiana	36 hours
New York, New York	26 hours
San Francisco, California	3-1/2 days
St. Petersburg, Russia	16 days
Vienna, Austria	11 days

28 In paragraph 5, <u>boarded</u> means to—

○ walk away

○ sit down

○ stand up

○ get on

29 Which sentence from the article is a fact?

○ *He knew how to build safe bridges, and he knew how to make the wheel safe.*

○ *Opening day of the Chicago World's Fair was in 1893.*

○ *The view of the city was spectacular.*

○ *Everyone wanted to go on the new ride.*

30 People at the fair were surprised to see the big wheel because it was—

○ not supposed to be built

○ in the middle of the fair

○ looked too dangerous

○ so enormous

31 According to the chart, from which place did it take the longest to get to Chicago?

○ Berlin, Germany

○ Edinburgh, Scotland

○ St. Petersburg, Russia

○ Vienna, Austria

32 According to the chart, from which two places did it take the same amount of time to get to Chicago?

○ Berlin, Germany and Vienna, Austria

○ New Orleans, Louisiana and New York, New York

○ London, England and San Francisco, California

○ Boston, Massachusetts and Montreal, Quebec, Canada

STOP

© Houghton Mifflin Harcourt Publishing Company. All rights reserved.

Writing: Revising and Editing

Read the introduction and the passage that follows it. Then read each question. Decide which is the best answer to each question. Mark the space for the answer you have chosen.

Juan is in the third grade. He wrote this story about a meal he made for his friends. Read the story and think about changes that could make the writing better. Then answer the questions that follow.

Juan Becomes a Cook

(1) I had been telling my friends about how much I like to cook. (2) The truth is, I've never really cooked anything. (3) I only knows how to make sandwiches.

(4) Last Saturday, my friends, Hector and Sammy, were at my house playing basketball. (5) Suddenly everyone was hungry. (6) Sammy said, "Hey, Juan, you like to cook. (7) Will you make us some lunch?"

(8) How could I say no? (9) I hurryed into the kitchen. (10) I looked in the pantry and the refrigerator. (11) Then I stopped to think for a minute. (12) Suddenly something occurred to me. (13) First, I grabbed some leftover cooked beans, apple slices, shredded cheese, lettuce, and dry cereal. (14) Then I threw in some spices that looked interesting.

(15) I crushed the cereal with a rolling pin and mixed it into the beans,

along with the apple slices and spices. (16) I put the mixture inside each

lettuce leaf. (17) Finally, I topped it with shredded cheese and rolled up

the lettuce.

(18) "What are these?" asked Hector when I served lunch.

(19) "The'yre good," said Sammy.

(20) Hector nodded. (21) "I guess you really do like to cook!" he said.

(22) What I am is a lucky cook! (23) I think I will stop stretching

the truth.

© Houghton Mifflin Harcourt Publishing Company. All rights reserved.

1 Which sentence could **BEST** be added at the beginning of this story?

- ⭕ My friends and I like to play basketball.
- ⭕ I like to make sandwiches for my friends.
- ⭕ My friends asked me to cook a meal for them.
- ⬤ Sometimes you get into trouble by stretching the truth.

2 What change, if any, should be made in sentence 3?

- ⬤ Change *knows* to **know**
- ⭕ Change *made* to **make**
- ⭕ Change *sandwiches* to **sandwichs**
- ⭕ Make no change

3 What change should be made in sentence 9?

- ⭕ Change *I* to **I'd**
- ⬤ Change *hurryed* to **hurried**
- ⭕ Change *kitchen* to **Kitchen**
- ⭕ Change the period to a question mark

4 What time-order word could **BEST** be added to the beginning of sentence 16?

- ⭕ First,
- ⬤ Finally,
- ⭕ Later,
- ⭕ Next

5 What change should be made in sentence 19?

- ⬤ Change *The'yre* to **They're**
- ⭕ Change the comma to a question mark
- ⭕ Change *said* to **say**
- ⭕ Change **Sammy** to *sammy*

GO ON

© Houghton Mifflin Harcourt Publishing Company. All rights reserved.

Read the introduction and the passage that follows it. Then read each question. Decide which is the best answer to each question. Mark the space for the answer you have chosen.

Jenna is a third-grader. She wrote this report about wind. She wants you to read the report and think about how she might correct and improve it. When you finish reading, answer the questions that follow.

What Is Wind?

(1) What is wind? (2) What causes it? (3) When sun shines on land and water, it warms them as well as the air above them. (4) The warm air becomes lighter. (5) As a result, it rises. (6) Then, cooler air rushes in to replace the rising warm air. (7) This movement creates wind.

(8) Earth's surface does not heat evenly. (9) As a result, wind blows

constantly. (10) Land heats and cools more quickly than water, so air is

always moving between land and water. (11) Places on Earth also heat up

and cool down at different rates, causing air to move between the hot and

cold places.

(12) Over time, wind can shape rocks and landscapes. (13) It blows

away tiny pieces of rock. (14) As a result, wind can reshape Mountains.

(15) The small, loose pieces of rock often form into sand dunes.

(16) They have learned to use the power of wind. (17) For example,

they use it to sail ships, dry clothes and fly kites. (18) Many citys use wind

power to generate electricity.

(19) We can't see wind, but we can feel it, see it's effects, and put it to

good use. (20) Day after day, wind is changing our world.

6 What change should be made in sentence 14?

○ Change *a* to **an**

○ Change *reshape* to **reshaped**

○ Change *Mountains* to **mountains**

○ Change the period to a question mark

7 What change should be made in sentence 16?

○ Change *They* to **People**

○ Change *have* to **has**

○ Change *learned* to **learn**

○ Change *power* to **pouer**

8 What change should be made in sentence 17?

○ Change *it* to *them*

○ Remove the comma after *ships*

○ Add a comma after *clothes*

○ Change *fly* to **flies**

9 What change should be made in sentence 18?

○ Change *citys* to **cities**

○ Change *use* to **uses**

○ Add a comma after *wind*

○ Change *electricity* to **Electricity**

10 What change should be made in sentence 19?

○ Change *can't* to **ca'nt**

○ Remove the comma after *effects*

○ Change *put* to **puts**

○ Change *it's* to **its**

STOP

Writing: Written Composition

> Write one part of your autobiography in which
> you tell about an important event in your life.

Use a separate sheet of paper to plan your composition. Then write your composition
on the lined pages that follow.

The information in the box below will help you remember what you should think about
when you write your autobiography.

REMEMBER—YOU SHOULD

❏ write about an important event in
  your life

❏ write in the first person

❏ include interesting and important
  details about the event in the order in
  which they happened

❏ use words and language that sound
  like you

❏ try to use correct spelling,
  capitalization, punctuation, grammar,
  and sentences

Name _____ Date _____

_____

_____

_____

_____

_____

_____

_____

_____

_____

_____

_____

_____

_____

_____

_____

_____

© Houghton Mifflin Harcourt Publishing Company. All rights reserved.

Name _____ Date _____

_____

_____

_____

_____

_____

_____

_____

_____

_____

_____

_____

_____

_____

_____

_____

_____

Reading

> Read the selection. Then read each question that follows it.
> Decide which is the best answer to each question.
> Mark the space for the answer you have chosen.

Cody and Friends Make a Difference

1   "Mom! Please don't throw away that bottle!" Cody called to his mother. He was seated at the kitchen table, writing on sheets of paper.

2   "What should I do with it, then?" Mom asked Cody.

3   "You should recycle it," said Cody. "That way it can be used again. If you throw it away, it'll become more trash."

4   "How did you become so wise about these things?" Cody's mom asked, taking a seat beside him at the table.

5   "We're learning about recycling at school," he answered. "The less we throw away, the less trash ends up in landfills or in the environment. Trash and pollution are global problems, and solving these problems begins with each one of us."

6   Cody continued, "We can reuse a lot of what we throw away. Used plastics can be made into all sorts of things such as rope and toys. Glass bottles and jars can be cleaned and used again, or they can be crushed and used in other products. Old newspapers can be made into cartons and bags."

7   "You're right," said Mom. "All of that is true."

8   "Then why were you going to throw away the bottle?" Cody asked.

9   "Our town doesn't have a recycling program," said Mom. "The city council doesn't think enough people would take advantage of it."

10   "I'll bet that a *lot* of people would recycle if we had a program. Someone ought to convince the city council to start one," said Cody. "I can't do it, though, because I'm just a kid," he said with a note of disappointment in his voice. He returned to his writing.

© Houghton Mifflin Harcourt Publishing Company. All rights reserved.

11   "What are you working on?" asked Mom.

12   "I'm writing a book report on *Charlotte's Web*," said Cody.

13   Cody's mother smiled. "Charlotte the spider saves Wilbur the pig," she said. "That is a great book whose story shows that even a small creature can make a huge difference."

14   Cody looked up from his writing. "Wait! Who says I can't make a difference just because I'm a kid? If a spider can save a pig's life, maybe anything's possible. There might be a way for me to start a recycling program after all. I could get my friends to help with the <u>project</u>."

15   "That's a great idea, Cody!" said Mom. "The next town meeting is in three weeks. You and your friends could make a presentation there. You could have your friends meet at our house this Saturday to make a plan."

16   On Saturday, 12 of Cody's friends met at his house. They discussed ways to make a presentation. There would be a lot of work, so they divided it into groups. Cody and some friends would write a letter asking the council to start a recycling program. Then, they would ask the town's residents to sign the letter. Others would <u>prepare</u> pictures, charts, and graphs to use during the presentation. Another group would gather things made from recycled materials that would show what recycling could do. <u>Finally</u>, everyone would try to get neighbors and family members to come to the meeting.

17   When the night of the town meeting arrived, the friends were a little nervous. "Now we will hear a presentation from some of the town's younger residents," announced the mayor. Cody presented the letter he and his friends had written along with several pages of signatures. The other <u>children</u> explained their pictures, charts, and graphs, and showed examples of objects made from recycled materials.

18   A month later, there was another town meeting. After the meeting, the mayor announced that the council had voted to start a recycling program. No one was more excited than Cody. The children's parents had a pizza party to <u>celebrate</u>. Cody gave a speech in which he thanked his friends for their help. At the end of his speech, he said, "Now I know that even a kid can make a difference, and 12 kids can make a *big* difference!"

GO ON

1   The author has Cody's mom throw away a bottle to show that—

   ○ Cody's mom is sometimes careless

   ○ Cody and his mother often disagree

   ○ Cody's town has no recycling program

   ○ Cody needs the bottle for a school project

2   Why does Cody want a recycling program in his town?

   ○ To clean up his neighborhood

   ○ To help reduce trash in the landfill

   ○ So he can sell used plastic and glass

   ○ So he can get an award from the mayor

3   In paragraph 5, the word pollution means—

   ○ new ways to use trash

   ○ trash that was put in landfills

   ○ waste that makes air, land, or water dirty

   ○ people who work to make a better world

4   In paragraph 5, the word global means—

   ○ serious

   ○ modern

   ○ difficult

   ○ worldwide

5   In paragraph 6, the word reuse means—

   ○ use up

   ○ use again

   ○ use before

   ○ use one time

6   What is the first thing that causes Cody to believe that he can make a difference?

   ○ The town meeting

   ○ Mrs. Reyna's idea

   ○ The book Charlotte's Web

   ○ The mayor's announcement

7   What does the word project mean in paragraph 14?

   ○ Party to celebrate

   ○ Contest on recycling

   ○ Report on what happens

   ○ Plan for work to be done

GO ON

8 Read the chart below and answer the question.

Talked
Spoke
Chatted

Which word belongs in the empty box?

- ○ Understood
- ○ Listened
- ○ Watched
- ○ Discussed

9 Why do Cody and his friends divide the work into groups?

- ○ There is a lot of work to be done.
- ○ There is not enough work for everyone.
- ○ They want to have a contest among the groups.
- ○ They want to make sure everyone has a job to do.

10 What does the word <u>finally</u> mean in paragraph 16?

- ○ In the middle
- ○ As a last thing
- ○ Without change
- ○ Lasting a long time

11 Which sentence from the story shows that many residents in Cody's town want a recycling program?

- ○ *Glass bottles and jars can be cleaned and used again, or they can be crushed and used in other products.*
- ○ *"I'll bet that a lot of people would recycle if we had a program."*
- ○ *Then, they would ask the town's residents to sign the letter.*
- ○ *Cody presented the letter he and his friends had written along with several pages of signatures.*

12 Which words from paragraph 18 help the reader know what <u>celebrate</u> means?

- ○ *had voted*
- ○ *was excited*
- ○ *had a pizza party*
- ○ *make a difference*

13 From the story, the reader can tell that Cody—

- ○ is always reading
- ○ will someday be a teacher
- ○ cares about his community
- ○ is the best student in his class

GO ON ➡

14 What is the author's purpose for writing this story?

○ To tell about ways to help the planet

○ To show how a town council meeting works

○ To show other uses for glass, paper, and plastic

○ To tell a story about some children who make a difference

15 Which word has the same sound as the underlined part of the word n<u>ew</u>spapers?

○ Powerful

○ Daughter

○ Unlawful

○ Blueberry

16 Which word has the same sound as the underlined part of the word coun<u>c</u>il?

○ Simple

○ Candle

○ Chicken

○ Bucket

17 Which word has the same sound as the underlined part of the word prep<u>are</u>?

○ Fair

○ Part

○ Hear

○ Card

18 Which of these shows the correct way to divide the word <u>children</u> into syllables?

○ chi • ldren

○ ch • ildren

○ chil • dren

○ childr • en

GO ON

Read the selection. Then read each question that follows it.
Decide which is the best answer to each question.
Mark the space for the answer you have chosen.

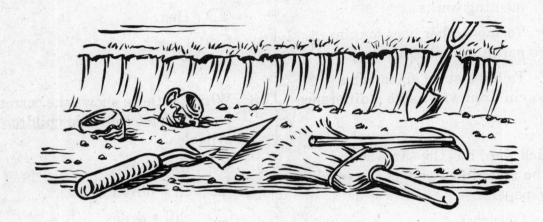

Journal Entries: My Week as a Fossil Hunter

Sunday, June 5

1   A dream has come true for me. Ever since I was five years old, I've been interested in dinosaurs. Now I have the chance to look for dinosaur bones. Tomorrow morning I'll be helping a team of students dig for fossils—and not just dinosaurs.

2   We're at a ranch in northern New Mexico. The climate is dry, the days are warm, and the nights are cool. There are cliffs, hills, and mountains. It is a beautiful part of the country. The dig site where I'll be working is called Hayden Quarry.

3   In the past few years, scientists and other <u>researchers</u> have found remains of dinosaurs, fish, and <u>traces</u> of other animals at the quarry. Thousands of animal bones are buried under the <u>rock</u> here. These bones and other objects tell us much about life long ago.

4   I hope I'm able to sleep tonight. I'm excited for tomorrow to be here. Who knows what we may dig up!

© Houghton Mifflin Harcourt Publishing Company. All rights reserved.

Monday, June 6

5   The first thing we have to do in our area is remove the rock that covers the fossils. This rock is called the "overburden." It comes from ancient rivers that flowed through the area.

6   We worked all day, using shovels to remove the rock. Halfway through our work, the sounds of a distant thunderstorm rumbled from far away. Our leader moved us to safety for a few hours. When the thunder stopped, we got back to work.

7   I asked our group leader how people knew to dig for fossils in this location. He told me that a hiker walking through here in 2002 discovered some fossils. After that, people who collect and study fossils began to come here to look for bones, teeth, and other prehistoric remains.

8   I must remember to take some pictures. The sunlight on the cliffs is so pretty!

Tuesday, June 7

9   Now that the rock layer is out of the way, we're using small picks and brushes to remove rock and dirt around the bones we find. We have to be very careful not to damage the bones as we uncover them. Some of the tools we use aren't much bigger than a toothpick!

10   I'm too tired to write any more tonight, but I loved every minute of today. The hard work and hot sun wore me out. It did help that I wore my hat and plenty of sunscreen. I wish I could stay for a whole month instead of just one week.

Wednesday, June 8

11   Today, one of the students found the upper leg bone of a dinosaur. Everyone was pretty excited about that discovery. I got to touch the bone with my hands! How many people get to do that?

12   The fossils we've been finding are very different in size. The fossils can be as tiny as a grain of sand or longer than one foot. To find the smaller fossils, we have to scoop up clumps of dirt and put them in bags that have very tiny holes. Next we put the bags in a nearby stream, under big rocks to hold them in place. The water washes the mud away. Then we dry what's left on a sheet in the sun. This makes it easier to find the smaller fossils.

13   I'm learning so much and having fun doing it. Maybe I'll do this for a living someday.

Thursday, June 9

14   So far our team has found six bones! It is amazing. Usually it takes months to find that many bones at one site.

15   All of the fossils will be sent to a lab. People at the lab will carefully study the fossils for <u>clues</u>. These clues tell them what animal the fossils belonged to, what it looked like, how it moved, and what it ate.

16   The bad news is that I am going home in two days. The good news is, when I get back home, I'll have lots of great stories and pictures to share with my family and friends.

---

19   The title of the journal helps the reader know that—

  ◯   the writer is a girl

  ◯   the writer is in New Mexico

  ◯   these are notes about looking for fossils

  ◯   these are notes about camping out in June

20   Which word from paragraph 3 helps the reader understand the meaning of <u>researchers</u>?

  ◯   *scientists*

  ◯   *remains*

  ◯   *dinosaurs*

  ◯   *animals*

21   Read the meanings below for the word <u>traces</u>.

traces \trā-š\ *noun*
1. trails
2. signs
3. straps
4. lines

Which meaning best fits the way <u>traces</u> is used in paragraph 3?

  ◯   Meaning 1

  ◯   Meaning 2

  ◯   Meaning 3

  ◯   Meaning 4

GO ON

22 The people are digging for fossils at Hayden Quarry so they can—

○ enjoy time outdoors

○ compare sizes of fossils

○ learn about life long ago

○ sell the fossils to make money

23 In paragraph 7, the word <u>location</u> means—

○ place

○ ground

○ town

○ way

24 How did people first learn that the area has many fossils?

○ A hiker discovered some fossils.

○ A newspaper article told of the fossils.

○ Scientists living in the area found the fossils.

○ Students on a field trip discovered the fossils.

25 The words below belong to the same category.

bones, fossils, teeth

Which of the following words names the category?

○ Plants

○ Remains

○ Tools

○ Rocks

26 What does the word <u>prehistoric</u> mean in paragraph 7?

○ After written history

○ Before written history

○ Related to history

○ The early part of history

27 The author organized the information in this journal—

○ by types of fossils

○ by days of the week

○ in order of importance

○ from last to first event

28 In paragraph 12, the word <u>clumps</u> means—

○ bags and tubs

○ rocks and stones

○ signs and fossils

○ lumps and clusters

29 Which sentence from the journal tells the reader that the dig at Hayden Quarry has been uncommon for scientists?

○ *A dream has come true for me.*

○ *The fossils we've been finding are very different in size.*

○ *Usually it takes months to find that many bones at one site.*

○ *All of the fossils will be sent to a lab.*

GO ON ➤

30 What does the word <u>clues</u> mean in paragraph 15?

- ○ Hints
- ○ Marks
- ○ Bones
- ○ Pictures

31 From the journal, the reader can tell that the person writing the journal entries—

- ○ is eager to get home
- ○ is a high school student
- ○ enjoys hunting for fossils
- ○ has been to New Mexico before

32 The author wrote this journal to—

- ○ explain how to dig for fossils
- ○ describe things to do at a ranch
- ○ tell about experiences at a dig site
- ○ persuade readers to search for fossils

33 Which word has the same sound as the underlined part of the word ro<u>ck</u>?

- ○ Camp
- ○ Chin
- ○ Knife
- ○ Voice

34 Which word has the same sound as the underlined part of the word rem<u>o</u>ve?

- ○ Took
- ○ Spoon
- ○ Wool
- ○ Good

35 Which of the following shows the correct way to divide the word <u>toothpick</u> into syllables?

- ○ too • thpick
- ○ too • th • pick
- ○ tooth • pick
- ○ tooth • pi • ck

Writing: Revising and Editing

Read each introduction and the passage that follows it. Then read each question. Decide which is the best answer for each question. Mark the space for the answer you have chosen.

Kevin is a third-grader. He wrote this draft in which he describes an experience. Read the paper and think about changes that could make the description better. Then answer the questions that follow.

Rolling on the River

(1) Have you ever weared a boat? (2) When my family and I was planning a trip to a kayak camp last summer, I learned about kayaks. (3) I found out that you actually wear them!

(4) A kayak is a type of boat, usually for one person. (5) Kayaks for the sea are long and thin, and kayaks for rivers are short and wide. (6) Our kayaks were river kayaks.

(7) Before you get into a kayak, you put on clothes that help to keep you warm and dry. (8) One piece of clothing is a skirt. (9) The skirt is rubbery. (10) The skirt fastens to a lip on the kayak to help keep water out of the boat. (11) After putting on the skirt, you squeeze into the

© Houghton Mifflin Harcourt Publishing Company. All rights reserved.

kayak and attach it. (12) This makes you feel like your wearing the

kayak. (13) For safety reasons, you also need to wear a helmet.

(14) For the first two days of camp, we learned what to do in case we

tip. (15) We did rolls under water, using our paddle to roll back on top of

the water. (16) We practiced these rolls in a swimming pool. (17) On the

third day, we paddled in our kayaks on the calm part of the river.

(18) Onse I got the hang of paddling, it was fun. (19) Each day, we

learned more about kayaking and paddled our boats on faster water.

(20) I liked the thrill of being on a fast-moving river. (21) I tipped over

into the river twice, but both times I rolled right back up!

GO ON

© Houghton Mifflin Harcourt Publishing Company. All rights reserved.

1 What change should be made in sentence 1?

- ☐ Change *Have* to **Has**
- ☐ Change *you* to **you've**
- ☐ Change *weared* to **worn**
- ☐ Change the question mark to a period

2 What change, if any, should be made in sentence 2?

- ☐ Change *and* to **or**
- ☐ Change *was* to **were**
- ☐ Change *learned* to **learn**
- ☐ Make no change

3 What is the **BEST** way to combine sentences 8 and 9?

- ☐ One piece of clothing is a rubbery skirt.
- ☐ One piece of clothing is a skirt rubbery.
- ☐ One piece of clothing is a skirt, a rubbery skirt.
- ☐ One piece of clothing is a skirt, the skirt is rubbery.

4 What change, if any, should be made in sentence 12?

- ☐ Change *makes* to **make**
- ☐ Change *feel* to **fell**
- ☐ Change *your* to **you're**
- ☐ Make no change

5 What change should be made in sentence 18?

- ☐ Change *Onse* to **Once**
- ☐ Change *I* to **me**
- ☐ Add a comma after *hang*
- ☐ Change *was* to **is**

GO ON

© Houghton Mifflin Harcourt Publishing Company. All rights reserved.

Read each introduction and the passage that follows it. Then read each question. Decide which is the best answer for each question. Mark the space for the answer you have chosen.

Jennifer is in the third grade. Her teacher asked each student to write about a favorite experience at school. This is a draft of Jennifer's paper. Read the paper and think about changes that could make it better. Then answer the questions that follow.

A Favorite Day at School

(1) We're learning about Italy in class. (2) Since food is an important part of life in Italy, our teacher invited a chef from an italian restaurant to come to class. (3) The chef showed us how to make fresh pasta.

(4) The chef began by mixing together flour, salt, and eggs to make pasta dough. (5) She kneaded the dough by folding and pressing it down. (6) She covered the dough in plastic wrap and let it rest for a while. (7) Next, she divided the dough into eight pieces and gave one piece to each pair of students. (8) Each pair had a metal pasta roller with a hand crank. (9) We put a piece of dough in one end and cranked it through. (10) What came out was a strip of dough. (11) It was flat. (12) We could change the roller setting to make the dough thinner and thinner. (13) When the strip were just right,

the chef cut it into smaller strips, like ribbons. (14) Then she boiled the

ribbons. (15) I used to think all pasta came from a box. (16) I couldn't have

been more wrong. (17) Welcome to homemade spaghetti!

---

6 What change, if any, should be made in sentence 2?

　　⬭ Change *is* to **are**

　　⬭ Add a comma after **important**

　　⬭ Change *italian* to **Italian**

　　⬭ Make no change

7 Which transition word could **BEST** be added to the beginning of sentence 6?

　　⬭ First,

　　⬭ Then,

　　⬭ Sometimes,

　　⬭ Although,

8 What is the **BEST** way to combine sentences 10 and 11?

　　⬭ What came out was a flat strip of dough.

　　⬭ What came out was a strip of dough, flat.

　　⬭ What came out was a strip of dough, it was flat.

　　⬭ What came out was a strip of dough and a flat dough.

9 What change should be made in sentence 13?

　　⬭ Change *were* to **was**

　　⬭ Remove the comma after *right*

　　⬭ Change *smaller* to **smallest**

　　⬭ Change *ribbons* to **ribons**

10 The **BEST** place to begin a new paragraph is before—

　　⬭ Sentence 3

　　⬭ Sentence 7

　　⬭ Sentence 14

　　⬭ Sentence 15

Writing: Written Composition

> Write an essay in which you try to persuade other third
> graders that it is important to get some exercise each day.

Use a separate sheet of paper to plan your composition. Then write your composition on
the lined pages that follow.

The information in the box below will help you remember what you should think about
when you write your composition.

REMEMBER—YOU SHOULD

❑ write to persuade others that it is
   important to get exercise

❑ use a separate paragraph for each
   reason and begin each paragraph with
   a topic sentence

❑ use convincing details that support
   your reasons

❑ use a closing sentence that sums up
   your goal and reasons

❑ try to use correct spelling,
   capitalization, punctuation, grammar,
   and sentences

© Houghton Mifflin Harcourt Publishing Company. All rights reserved.

_____

_____

_____

_____

_____

_____

_____

_____

_____

_____

_____

_____

_____

_____

_____

© Houghton Mifflin Harcourt Publishing Company. All rights reserved.

Name _____ Date _____

_____

_____

_____

_____

_____

_____

_____

_____

_____

_____

_____

_____

_____

_____

_____

96

Grade 3, Unit 4: Extreme Nature

© Houghton Mifflin Harcourt Publishing Company. All rights reserved.

Reading

Read the selection. Then read each question that follows it.
Decide which is the best answer to each question.
Mark the space for the answer you have chosen.

Anna's Adventure

1 Anna dressed in her new pants, tucked in her shirt, and brushed her hair. After she looked in the mirror and decided she was ready, she ran into the room where her parents were sitting.

2 "You look so lovely," her mother complimented her, smiling.

3 "Thank you," Anna said. "Can we leave now? I don't want to be late."

4 "Are you excited about seeing your favorite writer?" her father asked.

5 Anna grinned and nodded. Everyone knew how long she had been waiting for this day. She had read all the books written by Ms. Black and had even read some of them twice.

6 Ms. Black was a well-known writer who wrote mostly mysteries. Although the books were like written puzzles, Anna could usually untangle the mystery before the main character in the book did.

7 Anna and her parents drove to the bookstore, and fortunately, there was little traffic. Anna was surprised but pleased that they had arrived early because they found seats close to the front. All the chairs were taken soon after they got there. The crowd was composed mostly of young boys and girls, and everyone was discussing Ms. Black and their favorite books.

8 The crowd became still when the owner of the bookstore walked out. He welcomed everyone warmly, and then mentioned there was a small problem. Anna wondered what the hold-up might be.

9 "It seems Ms. Black is not here," he told the crowd.

GO ON

10   Everyone seemed disappointed. Anna was perplexed at first, but
then she remembered the plot of one of Ms. Black's books. In the book,
the main character was a writer, and the writer disappeared. Anna
tried to remember what had happened in the book and began glancing
around the room. A few other children seemed to understand that Ms.
Black might not really be missing after all.

11   Anna stood up and announced, "We have a mystery. Ms. Black is
missing, so let's figure out where she is."

12   The bookstore owner smiled, and the younger children in the crowd
calmed down. Anna and the older children formed a group and began
talking about where Ms. Black could be.

13   "What happened in Ms. Black's book about the disappearing writer?"
Anna asked.

14   One of the children replied, "The writer got lost in the library."

15   "Should we try to find her at the library?" another child asked.

16   "I think maybe she's here at the bookstore. Maybe she's lost among
the books here," Anna suggested. "Let's go look in the section where
the mysteries are."

17   The children walked through
the bookstore. Sure enough, sitting
comfortably among the mysteries was
Ms. Black, and she was reading a
book. The children gathered around
her in excitement. She told them
what a good job they had done, and
then she followed them into the room
where everyone else was waiting. The
crowd clapped when they saw her,
and Ms. Black smiled proudly.

18   "Thank you all for being here. I'm sorry I was late, but I suppose
I got a little lost. Perhaps you could clap again for the children who
solved tonight's first mystery," Ms. Black said.

19   The crowd applauded again and then settled in to listen to Ms. Black
read from her latest book.

© Houghton Mifflin Harcourt Publishing Company. All rights reserved.

1 The story mostly takes place at—
- ○ Anna's house
- ○ a writer's house
- ○ a bookstore
- ○ a library

2 In paragraph 7, what does the word <u>composed</u> mean?
- ○ Waited quietly
- ○ Sat in order
- ○ Be made up of
- ○ Listened carefully

3 What happens right after the bookstore owner says that Mrs. Black is missing?
- ○ The crowd seems let down.
- ○ The bookstore owner smiles.
- ○ Anna and her parents leave.
- ○ Anna decides she is ready.

4 How does Anna help solve the mystery?
- ○ Anna asks the children to find Ms. Black.
- ○ Anna remembers Ms. Black's book about a missing writer.
- ○ Anna tells the crowd to look for Ms. Black in the library.
- ○ Anna helps to calm down the younger children.

5 Ms. Black tells the children they did a good job because they—
- ○ are able to find her
- ○ read all of Ms. Black's books
- ○ come to listen to her speak
- ○ help calm down the young kids

> **Read the selection. Then read each question that follows it.**
> **Decide which is the best answer to each question.**
> **Mark the space for the answer you have chosen.**

The Running Farmers

1   Copper Canyon is located in Mexico. It is a large group of canyons or deep valleys that got its name from the copper-colored plants that grow on its walls. Copper Canyon is bigger and deeper than the Grand Canyon.

2   A group of Indians called the Raramuri live there today. Hundreds of years ago, different people moved into the area near Copper Canyon. The Raramuri wanted to be alone, so they moved to more hidden places. They moved deep into the canyons where many of them still live. Some live there part of the year and move to the top of the canyon for the rest of the year. They go back and forth to farm certain crops. Near the top of the canyon, they grow apples and peaches. In the canyons, they grow oranges and corn, which are their main foods.

3   It is hard to grow crops in Copper Canyon because the soil is not very good. For this reason, farms are far apart. The Indians have to find land where crops will grow. Homes are also far apart, so the Indians must travel a long way to work and to visit.

4   Raramuri means "foot runners." They run between their farms and their homes, and they run when they are herding their goats. They run when they are hunting, and they run when they carry supplies. They also play a game where teams kick a ball as they run. These races can last for days.

© Houghton Mifflin Harcourt Publishing Company. All rights reserved.

Name _____ Date _____

5   Some of the Raramuri Indians have entered running races in other parts of the world. All of the other runners wear professional running shoes. Sometimes the Raramuri wear running shoes, but other times they wear simple sandals. The bottoms of those sandals are made out of old tires, and still, the Raramuri can win the race!

6   Tarahumara, also known as Raramuri, is a language of Mexico. There are more than 60,000 Tarahumara speakers in Mexico. Look at the chart to learn some Tarahumara words.

English Word	Tarahumara Word
One	Biré
Two	'Osá
Three	Bikiyá
Four	Nawó
Five	Marí
Man	Rihóy
Woman	'Upí
Sun	Rayénari
Moon	Micá

© Houghton Mifflin Harcourt Publishing Company. All rights reserved.

Name _____ Date _____

6 The Raramuri moved deeper into Copper Canyon because they—

○ saw how beautiful the canyon was

○ knew it would be easy to grow crops there

○ did not want other people around

○ did not know where else to live

7 It is difficult for the Raramuri to grow crops because the—

○ soil is quite poor

○ canyon is so deep

○ Raramuri live far apart

○ Raramuri move often

8 Based on the article, how would a Raramuri child most likely go to a friend's house?

○ Ride a horse

○ Ride a bike

○ Walk

○ Run

9 What is the main reason the author wrote the article?

○ To show that Copper Canyon is bigger than the Grand Canyon

○ To describe the difficulty of farming near Copper Canyon

○ To tell a story about a Raramuri Indian who won a race

○ To give information about the Raramuri Indians

10 According to the chart, the Tarahumara word for "moon" is—

○ Marí

○ Bikiyá

○ Rayénari

○ Micá

11 According to the chart, the Tarahumaran word 'Upí means—

○ four

○ five

○ woman

○ man

GO ON →

© Houghton Mifflin Harcourt Publishing Company. All rights reserved.

Name _____ Date _____

> **Read the selection. Then read each question that follows it.**
> **Decide which is the best answer to each question.**
> **Mark the space for the answer you have chosen.**

Alice and Oskar

1   At lunchtime, Alice and Oskar share a meal. Alice eats muffins with butter and jelly, but Oskar prefers his muffins with honey.

2   After lunch, Alice and Oskar go for a walk. Alice walks on the trails in the park, while Oskar romps and runs among the trees. Sometimes Oskar scampers up a tree just to scare Alice a little. When he climbs down, Alice is always relieved. Then they walk some more.

3   In the afternoon, Alice and Oskar sit by the window and rock in Alice's special chair. Alice watches the cars go by and tells Oskar which cars they are, naming them one by one. "That's an old truck," Alice says, as she rubs Oskar's ears. "Oh, and look, there's a new van." Oskar just purrs.

4   In spring, Oskar helps Alice prepare her garden. They dig and plant flowers and vegetables. Oskar is very good at digging, but Alice is better at planting. When summer comes, Alice and Oskar like to work in the garden. Alice tends to her plants, while Oskar sniffs the special plants that Alice grows just for him.

5   On fall days, Alice rakes the colored leaves into large piles, and Oskar <u>pounces</u> into the piles, hiding under the leaves. On winter days they stay inside and listen to music. Alice sings along in her beautiful high voice, and Oskar just listens.

6   Each day, at dinner, Alice makes a nutritious meal. Alice eats with her fork and knife, Oskar licks his plate clean, and then they clean up the dishes.

7   After dinner Alice waters her plants, cleans up the house, and gets ready for bed. She and Oskar discuss their day and then hop into bed. Oskar warms up Alice as they drift asleep.

GO ON ➡

© Houghton Mifflin Harcourt Publishing Company. All rights reserved.

8   In the morning, they look at each other. Neither of them can remember a day without the other, for they are best friends.

9   They eat the same breakfast as usual and begin their day. They will eat their bread for lunch, they will go for a walk, and they will watch the cars go by. But best of all, they will always be together.

---

12   In paragraph 5, what does the word <u>pounce</u> mean?
○   Leap
○   Run
○   Climb
○   Walk

13   Which sentence best describes Alice?
○   She is very worried and nervous.
○   She does not know how to do much.
○   She is a kind and caring person.
○   She likes to be by herself.

14   Oskar scampers up a tree—
○   to scare Alice a little
○   because it is fun
○   to show how he can climb down
○   because Alice likes to watch him

15   Right after dinner, Alice—
○   cleans up the mess
○   looks at her garden
○   listens to music
○   hops into bed

16   The main reason the author wrote the story is to—
○   give information about gardening
○   show how different friends can be
○   tell a story about two friends
○   explain how some foods are made

> **Read the selection. Then read each question that follows it.**
> **Decide which is the best answer to each question.**
> **Mark the space for the answer you have chosen.**

Wonderful Bones

1   Do you know how many bones are located in your body? When you were a baby, you had about 330 bones, and now you have just over 200 bones. The number decreases because some bones join together as you grow. Your wonderful bones work together to protect you and support your body.

Many Uses

2   Many bones protect your body. For example, the bone that makes up your head is called the skull. The skull surrounds your brain and protects it from harm. The ribs that cover your chest protect your heart and lungs.

3   Other bones are used to support the body. The many bones in your feet allow you to walk and stand on your tiptoes. Finger bones move together so that you can throw a ball or tie a bow. Your hands and feet have more than half of the bones in your body! When you think of all that you do with your hands and feet, it's a good thing they have so many bones.

Biggest Bone

4   The longest and strongest bone in your body is in your leg. It is called the femur, and it goes from your hip to your knee. It is a very important bone because it carries all of your weight and helps you move from place to place.

Smallest Bone

5   Would you believe the smallest bone in your body is in your ear? It is about the size of a grain of rice and is called the stirrup. It is called that because it is shaped like a tiny loop and looks like the stirrups on a saddle. When sound waves come into your ear, the stirrup shakes back and forth, allowing the sound waves to reach your brain. When the waves reach your brain, you hear the sound.

GO ON

© Houghton Mifflin Harcourt Publishing Company. All rights reserved.

"Funny" Bone

6 Hah! The funny bone isn't really a bone at all. It is actually a nerve. When you hit the nerve that is near your elbow, it really hurts or tingles. What's so funny about that? The funny bone probably got its name from the bone that is above your elbow. That bone is called the humerus, which sounds like the word "humorous," meaning "funny."

7 The bones that make up our bodies are big, small, and in-between sized. They help us grow, <u>protect</u> us, and allow us to move. When you think about it, our bones really are wonderful.

---

17 The article is mainly about—
- ⬭ why we have fewer bones as adults
- ⬭ how different bones help our bodies
- ⬭ how the funny bone got its name
- ⬭ why the longest bone helps us move

18 In paragraph 7, what does the word <u>protect</u> mean?
- ⬭ Guard
- ⬭ Stand up for
- ⬭ Allow
- ⬭ Watch over

19 The skull and ribs are alike, because they both—
- ⬭ support the body
- ⬭ allow the body to move
- ⬭ are found in the chest
- ⬭ protect other body parts

20 Which section explains how bones help our bodies?
- ⬭ Many Uses
- ⬭ Biggest Bone
- ⬭ Smallest Bone
- ⬭ Funny Bone

21 Which sentence from the article states an opinion?
- ⬭ *Finger bones move together so you can throw a ball or tie a bow.*
- ⬭ *The longest and strongest bone in your body is in your leg.*
- ⬭ *Would you believe that the smallest bone in your body is in your ear?*
- ⬭ *When you think about it, our bones are really wonderful.*

22 According to the author, our bones are so wonderful because—
- ⬭ they send sound waves
- ⬭ some make us laugh
- ⬭ some look like other things
- ⬭ they protect and support us

GO ON ➡

> **Read the selection. Then read each question that follows it.**
> **Decide which is the best answer to each question.**
> **Mark the space for the answer you have chosen.**

Rainbow Trout's Colors

by Robert James Challenger
illustrated by Susan Kwas

1   Grandfather and his grandson were working outside, bringing in the winter firewood. The day was dull and rainy, and as they worked the cold water ran down their necks.

2   The grandson said, "I wish it would never rain. I like the clear sky and the warm sun better."

3   Grandfather looked at him and said, "Let's take a rest and I'll tell you a story about the rain.

4   They found a dry spot under Cedar Tree to sit, and Grandfather began.

5   Down in the lake, Trout once felt the same way you do. He liked summer's sun because food became more plentiful. This is when the water in the lake gets warm and the insects hatch.

6   One rainy day, Trout saw Eagle flying overhead and called out to him, "Eagle, can you fly up into the sky and drag the rain clouds away to the other side of the mountain?"

GO ON

© Houghton Mifflin Harcourt Publishing Company. All rights reserved.

7 Eagle asked, "So you think it would be good for the rain to go away so you could have sun all the time?"

8 "Oh, yes," said Trout. "It would be warm and bright and there would be lots of food for me."

9 Eagle thought, "It looks like I need to teach Trout a lesson."

10 Eagle flew up into the sky and dragged the grey rain clouds to the next valley, letting the bright sun shine down on Trout's lake.

11 Trout was very happy. Every day was bright, warm, and cheerful, and there was lots to eat. But after a while things started to change. Trout noticed that the water in the lake was not as deep as it used to be. The lake was getting smaller, leaving nothing but dry mud in its place. Trout also noticed that the insects, who needed the water to feed and hatch their eggs, had left. As the water got lower there was less to eat and Trout was finally trapped in a little pond with no food and barely enough room to turn around.

12 Trout looked up and saw Eagle watching him from a treetop. Trout called out, "Eagle, I was wrong. There can be too much sunshine. Now I know that rain is an important part of our world. Without it, the lake and everything I need to live will go away."

13 Eagle flew over the mountain and dragged the clouds back. Just before they covered over the sun, a bright rainbow came down from the rain clouds and shone on Trout. The colors splashed onto his scales and changed him into Rainbow Trout.

14 Grandfather looked up into the sky and said to his grandson, "I accept the cloudy weather, just like Rainbow Trout now does, because I know that without rain there would never be rainbows. Remember, everything has a <u>purpose</u>, even though we may not always understand what it is."

Name _____ Date _____

23 Grandfather tells his story—

- ○ under a tree
- ○ near a lake
- ○ in a boat
- ○ on a mountain

24 In paragraph 14, what does the word <u>purpose</u> mean?

- ○ Idea
- ○ Matter
- ○ Reason
- ○ Object

25 How are Trout and Eagle different?

- ○ Trout did not at first understand what is good about the rain, but Eagle did.
- ○ Trout noticed all the things around him, but Eagle did not.
- ○ Eagle was not bothered whether it rained or not, but Trout knew he needed rain.
- ○ Eagle did not have the power to stop the rain, but Trout did.

26 What happens to Trout when there is no more rain?

- ○ Trout's life gets easier because there is so much food.
- ○ Trout enjoys the sunny days and never complains.
- ○ Trout's lake becomes dry, and there is no food.
- ○ Trout decides to thank Eagle for taking the clouds away.

27 Which word best describes Grandfather?

- ○ Joyful
- ○ Wise
- ○ Hard-working
- ○ Careful

28 What lesson does Eagle teach Trout?

- ○ It is best when everything is warm and bright.
- ○ The sunshine brings food and warm water.
- ○ The clouds can be taken to another place.
- ○ Both sunshine and rain are necessary to live.

GO ON

© Houghton Mifflin Harcourt Publishing Company. All rights reserved.

Read the selection. Then read each question that follows it.
Decide which is the best answer to each question.
Mark the space for the answer you have chosen.

My Grandma Said

1   My Grandma is wise
    With sparkly brown eyes,
    And she told me this,
    "Hurt no living thing,
    My dear little miss."

2   Let the beautiful butterfly fly.
    Let the wild cat cry.
    Let the baby chick cheep.
    Let the stinky bug creep.
    Hurt no living thing.

3   Pick no pretty wildflower;
    Let it grow and <u>tower</u>
    Over other tiny plants.
    Cut no vine or rose,
    For each one grows
    In its dark, warm home of dirt.

4   Each animal and plant that is green
    Should be left to be seen
    By others who will <u>delight</u>
    In their animal ways,
    In their green plant sways,
    In all of their beauty so bright.

5   They are beautiful, like us.
    And so we must
    Never hurt any living thing.

© Houghton Mifflin Harcourt Publishing Company. All rights reserved.

29 According to the poem, why shouldn't wildflowers be picked?

- ⬭ So they can grow
- ⬭ So they will not spread
- ⬭ So their green plants can sway
- ⬭ So they can be food for animals

30 What does the author mean in the first four lines of stanza 2?

- ⬭ Don't be afraid of nature.
- ⬭ Leave nature alone.
- ⬭ Touch the creatures in nature.
- ⬭ Try to listen to nature.

31 What does the word <u>tower</u> mean in stanza 3?

- ⬭ To be high in the sky
- ⬭ To be taller than other things
- ⬭ A tall building
- ⬭ A jail or fort

32 In stanza 4, what does the word <u>delight</u> mean?

- ⬭ Enjoy
- ⬭ Live
- ⬭ Forget
- ⬭ Need

STOP

© Houghton Mifflin Harcourt Publishing Company. All rights reserved.

Writing: Revising and Editing

> **Read the introduction and the passage that follows it. Then read each question. Decide which is the best answer to each question. Mark the space for the answer you have chosen.**

Felicia is a third-grade student. Her teacher asked her class to write a story about a funny experience they had recently. Felicia wrote about playing a word game with her friends. Read Felicia's story and think about changes she could make to improve it. Then answer the questions that follow.

The Word Game

(1) Last week, Allie, Jan, Meena, and I played a word game. (2) We used small letter tiles to make words in crossword patterns. (3) For each word, we added up the points for each letter to figure out the word's score.

(4) Once we had used up all of our letters, the game was over.

(5) I played during Jan on one team against Allie and Meena on another. (6) After a few rounds, the two teams was tied. (7) Then, on Meena's turn, she spelled the word triplop.

(8) "If triplop is really a word, what does it mean?" I asked.

(9) "It means to gallop and trip at the same time," Meena answered weak.

(10) "You can't gallop *and* trip!" I said, giggling.

(11) Jan searched the dictionary for the word and finally announced,

"Triplop is not in the dictionary!" (12) We all laughed, including Meena.

Name _____ Date _____

(13) Near the end of the game, Meena tryed to use the word <u>qwerty</u> to win

the game.

(14) "That's the silliest made-up word you've ever played!" Jan said.

(15) Meena just smiled and handed Jan the dictionary. (16) When Jan found

the word, everyone except Meena was surprised. (17) With the points from

<u>qwerty</u>, Allie and Meena won the game.

---

1 Which sentence could **BEST** follow and support sentence 4?

- ○ Jan lives down the street from Meena.
- ○ The letters have points that go with them.
- ○ My friends and I like to ride bicycles together.
- ○ The team with the highest score would win the game.

2 What change should be made in sentence 5?

- ○ Change *played* to **plaied**
- ○ Change *during* to **with**
- ○ Change *one* to **won**
- ○ Change *on* to **under**

3 What change, if any, should be made in sentence 6?

- ○ Change *rounds* to **rownds**
- ○ Change *teams* to **team**
- ○ Change *was* to **were**
- ○ Make no change

4 What change should be made in sentence 9?

- ○ Change *It* to **She**
- ○ Change *and* to a comma
- ○ Change *answered* to **answer**
- ○ Change *weak* to **weakly**

5 What change should be made in sentence 13?

- ○ Change *Near* to **Neer**
- ○ Change *of* to **on**
- ○ Change *tryed* to **tried**
- ○ Change the period to a question mark

> **Read the introduction and the passage that follows it. Then read each question. Decide which is the best answer to each question. Mark the space for the answer you have chosen.**

Marcus is in the third grade. He wrote a story about his visit to a science museum. Read this draft of Marcus's story and think about changes that could make it better. Then answer the questions that follow.

Plan B

(1) Plan A, our picnic at the park, was cancelled because of rain.

(2) Mom said, "Let's try Plan B." (3) Our family always has a backup plan in case the first plan doesn't work out.

(4) Plan B was a visit to the Barger science Museum. (5) Is one of my favorite places. (6) You can see dinosaur bones, experience what it's like to be an astronaut, and take a make-believe journey through the solar system. (7) There are many other things to do at the museum, too.

(8) Dad and I visited an exhibit and the exhibit made us feel like we were in a fierce windstorm. (9) Later, my sister, Kayla, and I created music that was so good, other museum visitors applauded when they heard it!

(10) Kayla and Mom walked through the museums butterfly garden.

(11) Dad and I watched bees in their glassed-in hive. (12) We also watched a short film about how bees use danceing to communicate.

GO ON

Name _____ Date _____

(13) "I could spend a whole week at the science museum," Kayla said on

the way home. (14) "I think it should be our Plan A *and* Plan B all the time!"

---

6 What change should be made in sentence 4?

○ Change *was* to **were**

○ Change *a* to **an**

○ Change *visit* to **visits**

○ Change *science* to **Science**

7 What is the **BEST** way to rewrite sentence 5?

○ Is one, of my favorite places.

○ He is one of my favorite places.

○ The museum one of my favorite places.

○ The museum is one of my favorite places.

8 What is the **BEST** way to rewrite sentence 8?

○ Dad and I visited an exhibit, made us feel like we were in a fierce windstorm.

○ Dad and I visited an exhibit that made us feel like we were in a fierce windstorm.

○ Dad and I visited an exhibit and it make us feel like we were in a fierce windstorm.

○ Dad and me visited an exhibit and the exhibit made us feel like we were in a fierce windstorm.

9 What change should be made in sentence 10?

○ Change *Mom* to **mom**

○ Change *walked* to **walk**

○ Change *through* to **during**

○ Change *museums* to **museum's**

10 What change should be made in sentence 12?

○ Change *watched* to **wached**

○ Change *bees* to **bee's**

○ Change *danceing* to **dancing**

○ Change the period to a question mark

GO ON

© Houghton Mifflin Harcourt Publishing Company. All rights reserved.

> **Read the introduction and the passage that follows it.**
> **Then read each question. Decide which is the best answer to**
> **each question. Mark the space for the answer you have chosen.**

Tamara is a third-grader. She wrote this report about a program to protect Earth. She wants you to read the report and think about how she might correct and improve it. When you finish reading, answer the questions that follow.

Roots & Shoots

(1) Have you ever watched a plant grow? (2) If so, you know that a

network of roots holds a plant in the soil, and a tiny, green shoot is the first

sign of a new plant's life. (3) With out roots and shoots, plants could not grow.

(4) That's what Jane Goodall imagineed when she began the Roots &

Shoots program in 1991. (5) Goodall believes that young people can help

change the world. (6) Through Roots & Shoots, kids learn to spot problems

in their communities and think of ways to solve them. (7) Kids, teens,

GO ON

parents, and teachers can all work on service projects together. (8) Special

events to teach people how to care for Earth.

(9) Young people all around the world are joining Roots & Shoots

programs. (10) In some cities, kids are planting trees. (11) In others,

theyre volunteering at local zoos and animal shelters. (12) One kids are

helping to design Earth-friendly shopping bags. (13) "No matter how

many problems we face," says a teen volunteer, "there is still hope as long

as kids like us continue to care."

---

11 What change should be made in sentence 3?

- ○ Change **With out** to **Without**
- ○ Add a comma after **roots**
- ○ Change the comma to a period
- ○ Change **plants** to **Plants**

12 What change should be made in sentence 4?

- ○ Change **That's** to **Thats**
- ○ Change **Jane** to **jane**
- ○ Change **imagineed** to **imagined**
- ○ Change **in** to **below**

13 What change, if any, should be made in sentence 11?

- ○ Change **theyre** to **they're**
- ○ Change **zoos** to **Zoos**
- ○ Change **animal** to **animals**
- ○ Make no change

14 What change should be made in sentence 12?

- ○ Change **One** to **Several**
- ○ Change **are** to **is**
- ○ Change **shopping** to **shoping**
- ○ Change **bags** to **Bags**

15 Which of the following is **NOT** a complete sentence?

- ○ Sentence 7
- ○ Sentence 8
- ○ Sentence 9
- ○ Sentence 10

STOP

© Houghton Mifflin Harcourt Publishing Company. All rights reserved.

Writing: Written Composition

> Write a story about a character who solves an interesting problem.

Use a separate sheet of paper to plan your composition. Then write your composition on the lined pages that follow.

The information in the box below will help you remember what you should think about when you write your story.

REMEMBER—YOU SHOULD

❑ write about a character who solves an interesting problem

❑ include a plot with a clear beginning, middle, and end

❑ introduce the characters, setting, and problem at the beginning of your story

❑ include vivid details that paint a clear picture for the reader

❑ try to use correct spelling, capitalization, punctuation, grammar, and sentences

---

Name _____ Date _____

_____

_____

_____

_____

_____

_____

_____

_____

_____

_____

_____

_____

_____

_____

_____

_____

Name _____ Date _____

_____

_____

_____

_____

_____

_____

_____

_____

_____

_____

_____

_____

_____

_____

_____

_____

© Houghton Mifflin Harcourt Publishing Company. All rights reserved.

Reading

> **Read the selection. Then read each question that follows it.**
> **Decide which is the best answer to each question.**
> **Mark the space for the answer you have chosen.**

Being Good

1   Walter's <u>brother</u>, Morgan, was a star <u>athlete</u>. He was a great runner, a superb swimmer, and a fine baseball player. People who saw Morgan run, swim, and throw a baseball all said the same thing, "He's amazing. He makes it look so easy!" Of course, a person who makes something look easy has usually worked hard at it. Morgan was that type of person. He practiced every single day.

2   Walter admired his brother's ability to play sports and wanted to do what Morgan could do. He wanted to run like the wind, swim like a shark, and swing a bat like . . . Morgan.

3   Two things stood in the way of Walter's success, though. The first was that Walter didn't enjoy sports all that much, because he wasn't very good at them. The second was that he liked to spend his free time reading and writing stories. How would he find time to become good at running, swimming, and baseball?

4   In spite of these things, Walter announced to his family during dinner one night that he wanted to become good at sports. "I'm surprised to hear you say that. I didn't think you were interested in sports," said Mom when she heard the unexpected news. Dad looked at Walter with <u>disbelief</u>, and Morgan put down his glass of milk.

5   "You have to practice every day to be good, Walter," said Morgan. "How will you find the time, with your busy schedule?" Morgan continued, "My <u>advice</u> is to keep doing what you do well, which is writing stories."

6   Hearing this made Walter feel even more determined to prove himself in sports. He would work hard to <u>succeed</u>, and then people would praise him in the same way they praised Morgan.

© Houghton Mifflin Harcourt Publishing Company. All rights reserved.

7   The next day, Walter stayed after school and ran ten laps around the track. That night, after he finished his homework, he practiced swinging a baseball bat in the backyard. The following day was Saturday. When Walter woke up, his legs and arms were <u>sore</u>, but he went to the pool with Morgan anyway. He swam for an hour. Walter was so tired that he took a long nap when they got back home. When he woke up, he went running again and practiced throwing a baseball.

8   The next week, Walter did the same thing. His body ached all over, and he was tired most of the time. Mom and Dad were worried that he was trying too hard, so they had a talk with Walter. "Is this what you *really* want to do?" asked Dad.

9   "Well, it's not much fun," Walter admitted. "Morgan seems to enjoy sports a lot more than I do, but I want to be as good as he is."

10   "You're already good at something," said Mom. "You're a creative storyteller and an outstanding writer! You're already a <u>champion</u>, so why do you want to be good at something you don't enjoy?"

11   "People don't seem to care that much about writers," said Walter. "Do you ever see a <u>photograph</u> of a writer on a cereal box?"

12   "Walter," Dad said, "people do care about good writers, and, besides, you don't have to be good at everything."

13   Walter thought about what his parents were saying and realized that they were right. He decided to give up trying to be as good as Morgan at sports. The <u>decision</u> gave him a feeling of great relief, and he could almost feel his muscles get a little less sore.

14   A week later, Walter wrote a school essay about trying to be something he's not. Walter's teacher thought the essay was <u>excellent</u> and asked his permission to send the essay to a student <u>magazine</u>. Walter's writing appeared in the magazine a few months later. His classmates and family were very proud of him.

15   "I wish I could write as well as you can," said Morgan, smiling at his brother. "You make it look so easy!"

Name _____ Date _____

1 The word <u>athlete</u> in paragraph 1 means someone who—

    ◯ plays sports

    ◯ throws a ball

    ◯ does well in school

    ◯ practices every day

2 Why had Walter not succeeded in sports before?

    ◯ He did not enjoy sports very much.

    ◯ He spent his free time watching television.

    ◯ His parents did not want him to play sports.

    ◯ His brother would not teach him how to play.

3 In paragraph 4, the word <u>disbelief</u> means—

    ◯ trying to believe

    ◯ someone who believes

    ◯ the opposite of believing

    ◯ something to be believed

4 From the story, the reader can tell that—

    ◯ being good at sports requires practice

    ◯ most people are good at only one sport

    ◯ a person who tries hard enough will become good at sports

    ◯ being good at sports is more important than being a good writer

5 What does the word <u>advice</u> mean in paragraph 5?

    ◯ A guess about what will happen

    ◯ A wish for something to happen

    ◯ An opinion about what should happen

    ◯ An idea about what has already happened

© Houghton Mifflin Harcourt Publishing Company. All rights reserved.

Name _____ Date _____

6 Walter wants to be good at sports so that he can—

○ make new friends

○ have a healthy body

○ get praise from others

○ write about being an athlete

7 In paragraph 6, what does the word underline{succeed} mean?

○ Do well

○ Give up

○ Run fast

○ Work hard

8 In paragraph 7, the word underline{sore} means—

○ angry

○ hurting

○ sail high in the air

○ rise to a high level

9 Because Walter practices three sports, he—

○ has no time for his schoolwork

○ becomes tired and his body aches

○ gets better than his brother at the sports

○ becomes the fastest runner at his school

10 Why are Mom and Dad worried about Walter?

○ He is missing his friends.

○ He is not good at writing.

○ He is not helping enough at home.

○ He is trying too hard to be good at sports.

11 In paragraph 10, the word underline{champion} means a person who—

○ wants to be an athlete

○ wants to be good at something

○ is among the best at something

○ is the very first to do something

12 How does Walter change by the end of the story?

○ He gives up his plan to become good at sports.

○ He decides to practice only one sport every day.

○ He becomes more determined to be good at sports.

○ He decides to write about the sports he enjoys most.

Unit Test, Reading
© Houghton Mifflin Harcourt Publishing Company. All rights reserved.

124

Grade 3, Unit 6: Make Your Mark

13 In paragraph 11, the word <u>photograph</u> means a type of—

- ⬭ award
- ⬭ picture
- ⬭ writing
- ⬭ magazine

14 Morgan thinks highly of Walter's ability to—

- ⬭ run
- ⬭ swim
- ⬭ read
- ⬭ write

15 In paragraph 1, what is the last syllable in the word <u>brother</u>?

- ⬭ er
- ⬭ her
- ⬭ ther
- ⬭ other

16 In paragraph 13, what is the last syllable in the word <u>decision</u>?

- ⬭ on
- ⬭ ion
- ⬭ sion
- ⬭ ision

17 What shows the correct way to divide the word <u>excellent</u> into syllables?

- ⬭ exc • ell • ent
- ⬭ ex • cell • ent
- ⬭ exc • ell • ent
- ⬭ ex • cel • lent

18 Which word has the same sound as the underlined letter in mag<u>a</u>zine?

- ⬭ about
- ⬭ arch
- ⬭ almost
- ⬭ aim

GO ON ▶

© Houghton Mifflin Harcourt Publishing Company. All rights reserved.

Read the selection. Then read each question that follows it.
Decide which is the best answer to each question.
Mark the space for the answer you have chosen.

A Whole Other Country

1   Some people who have never visited Texas think the land is the same throughout the state. Some think the state is all desert filled with cactus. Others think it is an endless <u>plain</u>. Both are partly right. Texas has many deserts and plains, but those are just two types of the <u>impressive</u> land features found there. Texas also has mountains, forests, beaches, and canyons. The state is so large and so varied that some people use the <u>expression</u> "a whole other country" to describe it.

2   You can probably recognize the outline of Texas. Its shape is partly formed by water. In the north, the Red River forms the border between Oklahoma and Texas. The Sabine River <u>separates</u> Texas and Louisiana in the east. The Gulf of Mexico forms the southeast border of the state. The Rio Grande divides Texas from Mexico in the west and the south.

3   If you look at a map of Texas, you will see that eastern Texas has mostly plains and a few small hills. Western Texas has plains, hills, and mountains. The state has four main natural regions, or areas. The four regions are the Gulf Coastal Plain, the Central Plains, the High Plains, and the Mountains and Basins. The landscape of each region differs from that of the others.

Gulf Coastal Plain

4   The Gulf Coastal Plain region covers the eastern and southern part of Texas. It is the largest region in the state. The Gulf Coastal Plain runs along the Gulf of Mexico. The land here is mostly low and flat. Part of this region is tropical. You'll find miles of sandy beaches here. The region also reaches inland, away from the coast, for about 250 miles. Fields of vegetables and fruits grow to the west of the coast.

Name _____ Date _____

Central Plains

5   As you move away from the Gulf of Mexico, the land begins to rise. The Central Plains region is in the north-central part of the state. It has rolling hills and valleys. Many Texans call this region the Hill Country. <u>Cattle</u> and sheep graze on the grassy land there.

6   For hundreds of years, <u>ancient</u> rivers and streams shaped the land of the Central Plains. As you go farther west, there are forests of oak and hickory trees. Many different crops grow in this region.

High Plains

7   The High Plains are west of the Central Plains and are also part of the Great Plains of the United States. The land here is high and flat and looks something like a table. Parts of the High Plains are marked by long walls of steep cliffs and slopes. The southern and eastern parts are hilly. Many legends about rough, <u>tough</u> Texas <u>cowhands</u> are from the High Plains.

Mountains and Basins

8   This region is in western Texas. The land here is high, dry, and often rugged. The soil is dry and rocky. There are many small mountain ranges and <u>dramatic</u> cliffs in this region of Texas. These mountains are part of the Rocky Mountains, which stretch from Mexico to Canada. The highest <u>peak</u> in Texas is Guadalupe Peak. It rises nearly 9,000 feet above sea level.

9   A basin is land shaped like a bowl that has higher ground around it. In this region, the basins are parts of large deserts. You can visit Big Bend National Park in the Mountains and Basins region. You can also gaze at stars through a huge <u>telescope</u> at the McDonald Observatory in the Davis Mountains, which are also in this region.

The Land Called Texas

10   The state of Texas is varied and vast. It's no wonder that for centuries people have been drawn to this land. That may be why some call it a whole other country!

© Houghton Mifflin Harcourt Publishing Company. All rights reserved.

19 In paragraph 1, the word <u>plain</u> means—

- ⬭ easy to see
- ⬭ a flat area
- ⬭ not mixed with anything
- ⬭ a vehicle that flies in the sky

20 What does the word <u>expression</u> mean in paragraph 1?

- ⬭ A familiar saying
- ⬭ A symbol for an idea
- ⬭ A statement that is untrue
- ⬭ A person's first language

21 The outline of Texas is partly formed by—

- ⬭ hills
- ⬭ water
- ⬭ plains
- ⬭ mountains

22 In paragraph 6, the word <u>ancient</u> means—

- ⬭ moving swiftly
- ⬭ formed by the land
- ⬭ from a long time ago
- ⬭ flowing into the ocean

23 Which of these shaped the land in the Central Plains region?

- ⬭ Rivers and streams
- ⬭ The Gulf of Mexico
- ⬭ The Rocky Mountains
- ⬭ Grazing cattle and sheep

24 The word <u>cowhands</u> in paragraph 7 means—

- ⬭ fenced areas for cattle
- ⬭ ropes used for catching cattle
- ⬭ ranches where cattle are raised
- ⬭ people who take care of cattle

25 What does the word <u>dramatic</u> mean in paragraph 8?

- ⬭ Unusual
- ⬭ Dangerous
- ⬭ Causing wonder or awe
- ⬭ Having a variety of forms

26 In what region of Texas can deserts be found?

- ⬭ High Plains
- ⬭ Central Plains
- ⬭ Mountains and Basins
- ⬭ Gulf Coastal Plain

GO ON

27 What does the work <u>peak</u> mean in paragraph 8?

  ◯ Small hill

  ◯ Desert floor

  ◯ Grassy plain

  ◯ Mountain top

28 Which information belongs in the empty box?

┌─────────────────────────────────┐
│   **Features of the Central**   │
│   **Plains Region of Texas**   │
│ ┌───────────────────────────┐ │
│ │   Grassy land   │ │
│ ├───────────────────────────┤ │
│ │   │ │
│ ├───────────────────────────┤ │
│ │ Oak and hickory forests │ │
│ └───────────────────────────┘ │
└─────────────────────────────────┘

  ◯ Steep cliffs

  ◯ Rolling hills

  ◯ Low, flat land

  ◯ Sandy beaches

29 In paragraph 9, the word <u>telescope</u> means an instrument that helps you see objects that are—

  ◯ small

  ◯ nearby

  ◯ moving

  ◯ far away

30 Which sentence from the article states an opinion?

  ◯ *You can probably recognize the outline of Texas.*

  ◯ *The Gulf of Mexico forms the southeast border of the state.*

  ◯ *Many different crops grow in this region.*

  ◯ *A basin is land shaped like a bowl that has higher ground around it.*

31 From the article, the reader can tell that—

  ◯ few people live in the Central Plains region

  ◯ most people in the United States have visited Texas

  ◯ the High Plains region gets the most rainfall of all the Texas regions

  ◯ much of the land in the Mountains and Basins region is not good for farming

GO ON ➡

32 Which sentence from the article states a fact?

- ◯ *Some think the state is all desert filled with cactus.*
- ◯ *Others think it is an endless plain.*
- ◯ *The state has four main natural regions, or areas.*
- ◯ *That may be why some call it "a whole other country!"*

33 Which word has the same sound as the underlined letter in sep<u>a</u>rates?

- ◯ acorn
- ◯ around
- ◯ actor
- ◯ although

34 What is the correct way to divide the word <u>cattle</u> into syllables?

- ◯ ca • ttle
- ◯ ca • tt • le
- ◯ cat • tle
- ◯ catt • le

35 Which word has the same sound as the underlined part of the word t<u>ou</u>gh?

- ◯ such
- ◯ ouch
- ◯ watch
- ◯ caught

STOP

Writing: Revising and Editing

> **Read the introduction and the passage that follows it. Then read each question. Decide which is the best answer to each question. Mark the space for the answer you have chosen.**

Mita is in the third grade. Her teacher asked students to write about a celebration they enjoyed this year. Mita wrote about a special neighborhood event. Read the draft of her paper and think about changes that could make it better. Then answer the questions that follow.

Mrs. Cantu's Gift

(1) Our neighborhood is a large, friendly, and lively community. (2) More than 30 families live here. (3) Last month, something wonderful happened in our neighborhood. (4) We created a community garden! (5) Mrs. Cantu thought of the idea. (6) She has a backyard vegetable garden that everyone admires, and next to the house is a large piece of land that is her's.

(7) Not everyone has room for a garden," said Mrs. Cantu, "so let's build a garden that will benefit everyone in the neighborhood." (8) Mrs. Cantu taught music at our school until she retired last year.

(9) People in the community helped dig the garden, and Mrs. Cantu advised us about what to plant. (10) On Saturday March 3, everyone gathered at the garden to plant and water vegetable seeds. (11) Then

we had a huge celebration. (12) Mrs. Cantu made a speech, and we ate

sandwiches, apples and carrots for lunch.

(13) Families in the neighborhood will take turns caring for the

garden, and we will all share in the results. (14) What a great gift to

the community!

---

1 What change should be made in sentence 6?

  ○ Remove the comma after *admires*

  ○ Add a comma after *house*

  ○ Change *piece* to *peace*

  ○ Change *her's* to *hers*

2 What change should be made in sentence 7?

  ○ Add a quotation mark before *Not*

  ○ Add a comma after *room*

  ○ Remove the comma after *Mrs Cantu*

  ○ Change *let's* to *lets*

3 What change should be made in sentence 10?

  ○ Change *On* to *In*

  ○ Add a comma after *Saturday*

  ○ Remove the comma after *March 3*

  ○ Change *gathered* to **gatherred**

4 What change, if any, should be made in sentence 12?

  ○ Change *made* to **make**

  ○ Remove the comma after *speech*

  ○ Add a comma after *apples*

  ○ Make no change

5 Which sentence does **NOT** belong in this paper?

  ○ Sentence 3

  ○ Sentence 4

  ○ Sentence 8

  ○ Sentence 9

Read the introduction and the passage that follows it.
Then read each question. Decide which is the best answer to
each question. Mark the space for the answer you have chosen.

*Nicky, a third-grader, wrote this draft about an experience that she had.
Read the draft and think of ways to make the paper better. Then answer the
questions that follow.*

The Wild World Outside
My Window

(1) A week after we moved to Richmond Virginia, I caught the flu.

(2) Having the flu isn't fun, because your body feels tired and achy. (3) To

make it even worse, I had to stay in bed for several days.

(4) The first day, I read three books, but by the second day, I was bored

silly. (5) Then an interesting thing happened. (6) I noticed something flash

past my window. (7) I looked outside and saw a strange bird with a long

neck and long legs perched on a rock in our yard!

(8) "that's a blue heron," Mom said. (9) "They wade in shallow water

and catch fish with there sharp beaks." (10) Then, Mom and me watched

a squirrel chase another squirrel around the trunk of our walnut tree.

(11) Later, I saw three black crows hopping from tree to tree and six gray

birds hunting for worms on the ground. (12) Then, a brown rabbit with a white tail hopped out of the bushes and sniffed at a pile of leaves.

(13) Staying in bed wasn't so bad after all. (14) The squirrels, birds, and rabbit kept me from getting bored and showed me an exciting world right outside my bedroom window.

---

6 What change should be made in sentence 1?

- ⬭ Change *we* to **us**
- ⬭ Add a comma after *Richmond*
- ⬭ Remove the comma after *Virginia*
- ⬭ Change *flu* to **flew**

7 Which sentence could **BEST** be added after sentence 7?

- ⬭ I ate soup that Mom made.
- ⬭ I read my book for a while.
- ⬭ I called Mom into my room.
- ⬭ I saw an unusual bird with long legs.

8 What change should be made in sentence 8?

- ⬭ Change *that's* to **That's**
- ⬭ Change *blue* to **blew**
- ⬭ Remove the comma after *heron*
- ⬭ Change *said* to **say**

9 What change, if any, should be made in sentence 9?

- ⬭ Change *shallow* to **shalow**
- ⬭ Add a comma after *fish*
- ⬭ Change *there* to **their**
- ⬭ Make no change

10 What change, if any, should be made in sentence 10?

- ⬭ Change *Mom* to **mom**
- ⬭ Change *me* to **I**
- ⬭ Add a comma after *watched*
- ⬭ Make no change

GO ON

© Houghton Mifflin Harcourt Publishing Company. All rights reserved.

> ## Read the introduction and the passage that follows it.
> ## Then read each question. Decide which is the best answer to
> ## each question. Mark the space for the answer you have chosen.

Hamid is a third-grader. He wrote this draft of a report about Pluto. Read the paper and think about changes that could make his report better. Then answer the questions that follow.

From Planet to Ice Ball

(1) Pluto used to be one of the nine planets in our solar system but now it's just a small ice ball. (2) "There are finally, officially, eight planets in the solar system, says a scientist who studies the stars. (3) How does a planet get voted out of the club?

(4) Scientists made this decision at a meeting in 2006. (5) They voted and decided that Pluto is not a true planet. (6) First, though, the scientists had to agree on exactly what makes an object a planet. (7) Before 2006, they didn't have an official definition of a "planet."

(8) Now, scientists say that to be a planet, an object must meet three requirements. First, the object must orbit, or journey, around the sun. (9) Second the object must be large enough to have a round shape from the force of its gravity. (10) Third, the object must clear a path along their journey around the sun.

GO ON

(11) While Pluto meets the first two requirements, it has comets and
other things in its path. (12) Pluto is now called a dwarf planet. (13) Even
though it has been downgraded, it still enjois a special place in many
people's hearts.

---

11 What change should be made in sentence 1?

- ⬭ Change *Pluto* to **pluto**
- ⬭ Add a comma after *system*
- ⬭ Change *it's* to **its**
- ⬭ Add a comma after *small*

12 What change should be made in sentence 2?

- ⬭ Change *There* to **Their**
- ⬭ Add a quotation mark after *system,*
- ⬭ Add a comma after *scientist*
- ⬭ Change *studies* to **study**

13 What change should be made in sentence 9?

- ⬭ Add a comma after *Second*
- ⬭ Change *large* to **larje**
- ⬭ Add a comma after *enough*
- ⬭ Change *force* to **forced**

14 What change, if any, should be made in sentence 10?

- ⬭ Change *clear* to **clears**
- ⬭ Change *their* to **its**
- ⬭ Add a comma after *journey*
- ⬭ Make no change

15 What change should be made in sentence 13?

- ⬭ Add a comma after *though*
- ⬭ Change *enjois* to **enjoys**
- ⬭ Change *in* to **on**
- ⬭ Change *people's* to **peoples'**

Writing: Written Composition

> Write a composition to tell how to play a sport or
> a game that you enjoy.

Use a separate sheet of paper to plan your composition. Then write your composition on the lined pages that follow.

The information in the box below will help you remember what you should think about when you write your composition.

REMEMBER—YOU SHOULD

❑ write to tell how to play a sport or a game that you enjoy

❑ write a topic sentence that explains the main purpose of the instructions

❑ present the steps in their proper order, and include important details

❑ write a closing sentence

❑ try to use correct spelling, capitalization, punctuation, grammar, and sentences

---

© Houghton Mifflin Harcourt Publishing Company. All rights reserved.

_____

_____

_____

_____

_____

_____

_____

_____

_____

_____

_____

_____

_____

_____

_____

_____

© Houghton Mifflin Harcourt Publishing Company. All rights reserved.

_____

_____

_____

_____

_____

_____

_____

_____

_____

_____

_____

_____

_____

_____

_____

© Houghton Mifflin Harcourt Publishing Company. All rights reserved.

Name _____ Date _____

Donavan's Word Jar

> **Think back to the novel *Donavan's Word Jar* to answer questions 1–10. Mark the space for the best answer to each question.**

1 Donavan is a collector of—
- ⬭ buttons
- ⬭ coins
- ⬭ marbles
- ⬭ words

2 In Chapter 2, Donavan uses a dictionary to learn—
- ⬭ how pincers are used
- ⬭ what pincers look like
- ⬭ how to spell the word *pincers*
- ⬭ when the first pincers were made

3 In Chapter 2, Donavan learns that words—
- ⬭ can only be written
- ⬭ are always easy to spell
- ⬭ can be found everywhere
- ⬭ are always hard to understand

4 In Chapter 3, what is Donavan's problem?
- ⬭ He is late for school.
- ⬭ He cannot find his dictionary.
- ⬭ He cannot fit any more words in his jar.
- ⬭ He needs to keep his sister out of his collection.

5 Who suggests that Donavan start his own dictionary?
- ⬭ His sister
- ⬭ His father
- ⬭ His mother
- ⬭ His teacher

6 Chapter 4 takes place at—
- ⬭ Dad's new shop
- ⬭ Donavan's house
- ⬭ Grandma's house
- ⬭ Donavan's school

GO ON

© Houghton Mifflin Harcourt Publishing Company. All rights reserved.

Name _____   Date _____

7 Which of the following sentences helps the reader visualize that Nikki is sick?

○ *On her lap sat a large box of tissues.*

○ *Donavan always had to tell Nikki things.*

○ *She laughed and asked, "Donnie, is that a real word?"*

○ *Donavan opened the door to Nikki's room and peeped in.*

8 In Chapter 5, why does Donavan make Nikki promise to give back the word she picks out of his jar?

○ He knows she cannot read.

○ He is worried she will keep it.

○ He is afraid he will catch her cold.

○ He does not want her to draw on the paper.

9 In Chapter 6, who does Donavan go to see for help with his problem?

○ His father

○ His friend

○ His teacher

○ His grandmother

10 When Grandma sees Donavan's word jar, she—

○ feels proud of him for his collection

○ thinks collecting words is silly

○ gets angry that he wastes his time collecting words

○ tells him he should share his word collection with others

Jake Drake, Know-It-All

Think back to the novel *Jake Drake, Know-It-All* to answer questions 1–10. Mark the space for the best answer to each question.

1 Jake's favorite thing to do is—

  ⬭ read mysteries

  ⬭ use a computer

  ⬭ cook good things to eat

  ⬭ play sports with his friends

2 Which word does Jake use to describe himself?

  ⬭ Awkward

  ⬭ Greedy

  ⬭ Lazy

  ⬭ Smart

3 Which of the following sentences from Chapter 2 helps the reader visualize what Mrs. Karp looks like?

  ⬭ *I thought maybe he worked for a circus.*

  ⬭ *Every kid in school knows how loud she can yell.*

  ⬭ *He was wearing a yellow sport coat and a purple tie with green polka dots.*

  ⬭ *But standing up on the stage that morning in a green dress, she looked like a giant piece of celery.*

4 Which detail shows that Mr. Cordo is scared to talk to the students?

  ⬭ He is sweating.

  ⬭ He thanks Mrs. Karp.

  ⬭ He says he is glad to be there.

  ⬭ He has to pull the microphone down.

5 Mr. Cordo gets the students excited about the science fair by—

  ⬭ telling them they will be on TV

  ⬭ promising to give them a grand prize

  ⬭ offering them a job at his store

  ⬭ saying he will give them money for each project that is entered

6 Chapter 3 is mostly about—

  ⬭ how to make a rocket

  ⬭ the rules for the science fair

  ⬭ how a computer game works

  ⬭ the things Jake talks to his family about

© Houghton Mifflin Harcourt Publishing Company. All rights reserved.

7 In Chapter 5, what happens when Jake's dad suggests that he build a rocket?

    ◯ Jake asks if he could go to the library to do some research.

    ◯ Jake gets excited because he thinks the judges will like that idea.

    ◯ Jake says he does not like the idea because it will be too much work.

    ◯ Jake tells him he cannot make anything that burns, smokes, or explodes.

8 In Chapter 6, what does Jake pick for his project?

    ◯ Building a rocket

    ◯ Watching how ants live

    ◯ Making an electromagnet

    ◯ Growing different kinds of plants

9 In Chapter 7, how does Jake show he is clever?

    ◯ He keeps the secret that his sister Abby broke a statue.

    ◯ He makes a list of all the things that are in his junk drawer.

    ◯ He lets other students see him with things that have nothing to do with his project.

    ◯ He lets Kevin stand behind him when he gets in line to turn in his permission slip.

10 Who wins first place for the third grade at the science fair?

    ◯ Jake

    ◯ Kevin

    ◯ Marsha

    ◯ Pete

STOP

Name _____ Date _____

Capoeira

> ## Think back to the novel *Capoeira* to answer questions 1–10. Mark the space for the best answer to each question.

1 According to legend, capoeira was created by—

- ⬭ African slaves
- ⬭ Brazilian children
- ⬭ Native Americans
- ⬭ Portuguese explorers

2 Why did capoeira players use nicknames in the late nineteenth century?

- ⬭ The game was illegal.
- ⬭ It made the game more fun.
- ⬭ The game was only for adults.
- ⬭ It allowed the children to practice their Portuguese.

3 While playing, capoeiristas can touch the floor with their—

- ⬭ back and sides
- ⬭ shoulders and elbows
- ⬭ hands, feet, and head
- ⬭ arms, legs, and stomach

4 The reader can conclude that capoeira moves—

- ⬭ are never used in fighting
- ⬭ can only be done by children
- ⬭ look like the thing for which they are named
- ⬭ are always named after some kind of living thing

5 Which of the following sentences states an opinion?

- ⬭ *The ginga is a springboard for the many movements that follow.*
- ⬭ *When two players start a game they face each other and step from side to side and forward and back in a kind of dance.*
- ⬭ *The object of the game is to put one's opponent in a position where he or she could be taken down with a sweep, kick, or blow.*
- ⬭ *Capoeiristas are playful and respectful as they move in continuous sequences from attack to defense and back to attack.*

Novel Test
© Houghton Mifflin Harcourt Publishing Company. All rights reserved.
145
Grade 3, Unit 6: Make Your Mark

Name _____ Date _____

6 People who play capoeira must be—
- ⬭ very tall
- ⬭ good singers
- ⬭ able to run fast
- ⬭ able to move easily

7 Which of the following sentences helps the reader visualize what a berimbau is?
- ⬭ *The berimbau is used to direct the capoeira games.*
- ⬭ *After teaching the students the song, Malandro begins to play an instrument called a* berimbau.
- ⬭ *The berimbau is a long wood bow with a steel wire and a hollowed-out gourd near the bottom.*
- ⬭ *In nineteenth-century Brazil berimbaus were also used by peddlers to announce their arrival in town.*

8 Before two players at Mandinga Academy begin to play the game, they—
- ⬭ hold hands
- ⬭ sing a song
- ⬭ clap loudly
- ⬭ hug each other

9 Which word tells the reader that this sentence states an opinion?

> *The players have fun and try to make their moves graceful, like a dance.*

- ⬭ Dance
- ⬭ Fun
- ⬭ Like
- ⬭ Moves

10 Which word from the book is used to state an opinion?
- ⬭ Cities
- ⬭ Discover
- ⬭ Practice
- ⬭ Thrill